WHERE DARKNESS REIGNED

Remnant
Publications

Greg Emelander

Published by
Remnant Publications
649 East Chicago Road
Coldwater MI 49036
www.remnantpublications.com

The author assumes full responsibility for the accuracy of all facts and quotations as cited in this book.

Cover design by David Berthiaume

ISBN: 978-1-629130-70-5

TABLE OF CONTENTS

Introduction

This book wasn't written to be a best seller or to pander to some organization's agenda. This book was written for the sole purpose of reaching those who have found themselves in a place where life seems to have lost its purpose. *Where Darkness Reigned* is the story of a young man who, though raised in a Christian home and educated in Christian schools, found himself facing 20 to 30 years in prison within a few short years of abandoning his faith. The story could have ended there, and it would have been an impressive cautionary tale, but it didn't.

Most individuals who have been through what Greg has usually find themselves bound by the restrictions that society places on them. Labeled a felon, drug addict, and all-around dangerous individual, Greg knew that his future, if left in his own hands, was going to be filled with disappointments and discouragement.

Once the drugs had been eliminated from his system, Greg was confronted with the reality of not only who he was, but what he had become. As a child, he had been one of the privileged few to go to a church school, to have parents who loved him, and to have a future as limitless as the sky. As an adult, he was faced with the consequences of the choices that he had made and those consequences were so dark and hopeless that many men and women who face similar futures take their own lives in an effort to speed up what they feel is the inevitable outcome. However, Greg was shown something that many of those individuals never discover.

Greg saw that God not only existed, but that He had been relentlessly pursuing him, even when Greg was living in full rebellion. Through that he saw that there was a way to find, not only the hope and happiness that he had sought through drugs, money, and power, but also how to fully restore his life. By following the path in front of him, he could see that his past did not have to dictate his future.

Where Darkness Reigned is the story of how Greg went from being a six-time convicted drug trafficker, home invasion specialist, armed robber, and extreme drug addict, to being a successful professional in a field that he never imagined being in. What is so important about Greg's story is that every positive thing that has happened in his life is entirely possible in yours.

Chapter 1

BEGINNINGS

I wasn't born an armed robber, drug dealer, or cold-blooded shooter. I never planned on becoming a six-time convicted felon, drug addict, or home invasion specialist. I never dreamt of becoming one of West Michigan's most wanted criminals; yet all of these things would, in one way or another, eventually come true. To look at me in my youth you would have seen nothing more than a typical Christian country kid. You would have seen a young boy with dreams of becoming an adventure-seeking woodsman, living in the wilds of the Rockies or Alaska. From an early age, on any given afternoon, you could find me wandering through the woods with a BB gun, imagining that I lived in an era that died away long ago.

My beginnings were much like many other children who grew up in a religious home. My older brother, younger sister, and I attended the local church school, and we all did our best to succeed. Our teachers were determined to provide the best education that they could possibly give, and it showed. By second grade I was reading and writing at a grade level that was higher than average, writing cursive proficiently, and playing virtually any song on the piano by ear. I wasn't unique though; many of the students in our school could do what I could, and some of them excelled far beyond me. God was at the very core of our instruction, and the Bible was our main textbook. The world was truly at my fingertips. I could have been anything that I put my mind to, and I knew it.

For the most part, my siblings and I obeyed our parents, did our schoolwork, and completed our chores at home. Apart from the occasional expression of youthful ignorance, we were considered good kids. There was nothing that would indicate that I would end up being the person that

I later became. From our perspective as children, we had the perfect life. Though I'm sure there were always things that we wanted, there was never a time when we didn't have something that we needed. Our parents regularly sacrificed their own needs to make sure that we children never went without.

Life was good for many years. My life, a life that had been extremely happy, gradually started to change as the years went by. We didn't see it immediately, because as many children are, we were focused on ourselves. By the age of 12 the changes were clearly visible. I could sense a lot of stress in the home, and almost overnight we stopped talking to each other the way we had before. Sure we had gotten into arguments in the past, but things were somehow different. We all began responding to the changes by acting out against each other and against our parents. Eventually my parents began to argue in front of us, which they had rarely done in the past. After we went to bed at night, it would only get worse. My brother and I would go over to the register on the floor, put our ears up to it and try to listen to what they were saying as they argued.

Though we knew things had been different lately, we never realized what was coming. We had never thought that anything serious would come from the arguments that my parents had, but we kids didn't know how deep the wounds were between the two of them. The day finally came when my parents made the decision to separate. Though they said they were going to try to work things out, there was a sense of finality in the air—like the divorce had already happened.

Within a few weeks, we were being tossed back and forth from one home to another. Confusion and disorientation followed the chaos that emanated from within our home. My family, the one thing that supported me and afforded me stability had been uprooted, and all that was once good and right in my life soon became uncertain.

Strangely enough, my parents never told us why they had decided to separate, but I could tell that it wasn't good. The abrupt nature of the announcement took us all by surprise. Matter of fact, it wasn't until quite recently that I actually learned all of the facts that surrounded the events of my parents' divorce, but let it be said that the incidents that brought it about were anything but typical. Everyone—our family, our friends and even our church—was severely affected by their decision.

Prior to the separation we had lived on a picturesque farm in the countryside six miles away from any town. We were surrounded by the beauty of nature and were blessed not only to have cherry and pear trees in the front yard, but also, each spring, our raspberry and blackberry bushes would produce the sweetest berries that I have ever tasted.

It's amazing how destructive a divorce can be. The divorce changed a lot of things, and where we lived was one of those things. My entire life had been spent on that little farm. All of my childhood memories were associated with that house; and with one stroke of a pen, all of that was wiped away. But what could we do? My brother, sister, and I were doing our best to stay out of it as much as possible. If that meant that our childhood home would have to be sold, then so be it. By my fourteenth birthday, the divorce was finalized. My sister and I had moved to a new home in the small village of Saranac, Michigan with our mother while my older half-brother moved in with his father.

Saranac was a small community six miles south of where I had grown up. In a lot of ways it resembled the town of Mayberry made popular by a show produced in the 1950s called *The Andy Griffith Show*. The house my mom bought was practically brand-new. It had five bedrooms, two and a half baths, and it sat on a lot that was nearly two acres. The property itself was smaller than I was used to, but at least it wasn't located directly in town. The home my mom bought was located on a dirt road that was only a quarter of a mile away from the village limit.

Where we lived wasn't the only thing to change though; many things changed with the divorce. For years we had attended church school in a one-room schoolhouse, but with the divorce came the fact that we would have to switch schools. There had been so much gossip surrounding the divorce that none of us children could attend school without having someone say something inappropriate. Ultimately, we were enrolled in the local public school in Saranac called Harker Middle School. And with that move, my life and my personal identity were thrown into a tailspin.

Everything that I had once identified myself with was no longer present. I was faced with having to identify with a culture that I had once been taught to distance myself from. I became confused and conflicted. It was the perfect environment for the devil to do his work, and he didn't hesitate to jump at the opportunity.

With the move to a new school came new friends. I had grown up going to a church school so my social skills in a worldly atmosphere were anything but stellar. I was awkward, skinny, and kind of nerdy-looking, but in many ways that became my advantage. Many people underestimated me. I may have been awkward and a little nerdy, but I was calculating and highly intelligent, as are most criminals.

As I adjusted to my surroundings, I began observing those around me. I watched the jocks, the gothic kids, the preppy kids, and all I saw were people that I did not fit in with. I didn't know who I really was; all I knew is that I was not like them. Eventually, I found myself hanging out with three particular individuals. My circle of friends soon became Joe, Harold, and Josh. They weren't jocks, they weren't academics, nor were they preppy. They were the guys who weren't afraid to pick up a baseball bat and put it upside someone's head. I can recall several after-school fights where 50 to 75 kids would encircle us for the big event. Even though we were only 14 years old and living in a small town, we were engaging in fights usually only seen in big cities. My friends and I didn't have a problem taking it to the next level. While most of our group would deal with things in a physical manner, I was more calculating in how I dealt with issues. I was the type of individual to utilize explosives, arson, and other non-traditional means of revenge. As a team we were a formidable opponent.

My school life wasn't the only thing in chaos. The home that we had moved into, unbeknownst to us, had been owned by the neighbor's father. He had sold the land because of financial issues, and the son had a difficult time accepting the loss of the property. Making this situation even more difficult is the fact that this man's son was mentally unstable. He was convinced that the land was rightfully his, and within a few weeks, he began stalking my mother and young sister in an attempt to get us to move away. He thought that if we moved, he would get the land back.

It started out with inappropriate phone calls but quickly escalated to him breaking into our home when we were gone. At night, he would harass us by messing around with the doorknobs and windows. Once we had proof that he was making entrance into our home, my mother obtained a personal protection order, and we began arming ourselves. She had her pistol and I had a 20-gauge with a pistol grip. We both slept with loaded weapons at our sides, that is, when we were able to sleep.

The next few months were a mix of attempted break-ins, 911 calls, and even an attempted abduction. The guy showed up at my high school and tried to abduct me in front of everyone. I was able to pull away from his grasp and board my bus. The driver called the police, and once we left the school she made the decision to reverse the route, which meant that I would be dropped off at home first instead of last. As we pulled up to my driveway, I witnessed the local sheriff's department arresting him in his front yard. He was sentenced to 60 days in jail and upon his release, the terror resumed.

As the months went on I lost weight and my grades suffered. I couldn't sleep because he would make noises outside of our house in order to provoke us. One day, everything came to a head. After nearly 90 days of repeated 911 calls, we had had enough. He tried breaking into the lower level of our home through a pair of French doors that went from a large bedroom to the back-yard. I woke up and quietly notified my mom. Silently we dialed 911, set down the phone, and crept through the house towards the deck that sat above the area where the intruder stood. For the last few weeks I had been sleeping on my mother's bedroom floor with gun in hand hoping that if he made entry I would have the ability to intervene. We were both tired of being the victims. Up until this moment we had always been the prey and he the predator, but that was about to change in a very dramatic way.

We quietly unlocked the door and then burst out onto the deck, catching him completely off guard. My mom fired her .38 at him. She took two shots, but they missed their mark. He ran as fast as he could across the yard, and as he ran I leveled my shotgun at him. Once I thought I had him in my sights I squeezed the trigger and my 20-gauge thundered in the quiet of the night. Just as I let loose, the state police arrived in force. The cruisers came flying through our lawn from multiple directions. For weeks they had been responding to our calls for help and fortunately on this night they had been at a restaurant just two miles down the road

Upon arrival the police observed the neighbor crawling to his door. He hadn't been struck by my mom's .38 caliber pistol, but by the load that I had in my shotgun. Ultimately, thanks to the copious amount of police reports that had been recently amassed, the prosecutor ruled the incident "self-defense" and criminal suspicion was lifted from me, but something in me changed that evening. A line was crossed within myself that many people never experience. Once you have taken that step, you can't undo it. I had a man at the end of my barrel, and I pulled the trigger with a complete understanding of what the consequences were. I knew the power of that weapon and since I had hunted before, I was fully aware of the damage it would inflict. Something died in me that night. Even though we finally felt safe, I knew that I would never be the same.

Our family had decided to do their best to keep the events of that night a secret, but the months of anxiety, fear, and stress had taken their toll. My teachers began commenting on the changes in my attitude and behavior. Slowly but surely, my rebellious attitude increased. I isolated myself from my family and even many of my friends. My life, which had seemed to be on a continual downward spiral, just continued to degrade in ways that I never imagined possible. The young man—who used to be a sincere Christian—over time, became a manipulative person who preyed on the vulnerable or unsuspecting.

By the age of 15 I was smoking two packs of cigarettes, and by the age of 16 I had incorporated weed. Occasionally, I'd even smoke some hash. True to form though, I wasn't satisfied with the weed. I always went beyond the boundaries of moderation. On the weekends I would buy alcohol and call my friends over to get drunk and high.

Every Friday when school got out, some older friends would purchase a gallon of vodka for me, and as a mixer I would buy a couple gallons of orange juice or Ruby Red Squirt. Once the drinks were put on ice and the cups distributed, my friends and I would get the party started. Usually we would drink in different locations, but where we were mattered very little once the alcohol started flowing.

You would think that my age and background would have affected my attitude, but I knew how to get in trouble with the best of them. By now my Christian upbringing was undetectable by those around me. I had traveled so far down the "path of acceptance" that those who had known me before could barely recognize me. I had kicked religion out of my life and Christ completely out of my heart. No matter what I did, no matter how bad it was, I was no longer under conviction for my sins. I had numbed the pain, the anger, and the resentment that had built up within. All that I cared about was me, myself, and I. With all that was happening in my life, it was only a matter of time before the police would be coming down on me.

Not long after the incident with my neighbor, a local kid approached my friends and I and asked us for a bag of weed. Nobody really knew the kid and so we also didn't have any intention of giving him any real weed. However, we weren't going to let this opportunity pass us by. We saw this as an easy way to make some money by giving him a counterfeit that cost us nothing. Had I given him real weed, we would have made a fourth of the amount of profit than we would have otherwise.

It wasn't like we had fake weed just lying around. In order to have something to sell, we went to my mother's house and gathered every type of plant that we could find growing in her tree line that resembled bud. In order to mimic the seeds, I used the dried seed from the crushed red pepper that she had in the kitchen. We put it all in a bag and when it was all meshed together, it actually looked pretty convincing—at least it did at first glance. If you looked at it for more than one or two seconds it was obvious to anyone who had smoked weed that it wasn't real.

We went over the plan, called him and told him where to meet us, and then climbed in the car. When we rolled into town, we were a couple of minutes early so I decided to stop at the gas station in order to get some beef jerky. We finished getting our snacks and headed back down the street.

That day, there were five of us crammed into my car. As soon as we pulled out of the gas station parking lot, I noticed a police cruiser on my tail. It wasn't but a few seconds later that his overhead lights and siren came on. I continued driving a short distance until we were in front of a friend's home. We pulled into my friend's driveway and the game of cat and mouse began.

I watched as the officers slowly approached my car from both sides. The one approaching from behind the driver's side motioned to his partner to pay special attention to what we were doing inside. The officer came up to my window, asked for my license, registration, and proof of insurance. He went back to the cruiser and ran my plates. When he came back, he told me that when he had first approached the car he had smelled what appeared to be the smell of weed. I couldn't help but laugh out loud when he said that. I informed him that what he smelled was nothing but beef jerky. He wasn't impressed by my comment or the smile that accompanied it. About 50 seconds later, I was admiring my new set of bracelets while sitting in the back of the cop car.

The officers searched my vehicle and came back to their car, strutting like they had just secured a victory for "the good guys." As I sat in the back of the cruiser, I saw the younger of the officers open the bag. He smelled it and confidently proclaimed, "This is some strong weed!"

I countered by laughing. He turned and scowled at me. I asked him if he had ever even seen weed. I told him that what he had in that bag was nothing

11

but herbs from my mother's tree line and kitchen cabinets. The more experienced officer grabbed the bag, smelled it, and then looked at me in the rearview mirror, shaking his head. He then opened his door, got out and opened my door. He told me to get out and turn around. As I turned around, he grabbed my hands and started releasing me. Once the cuffs were off, he made it clear that he could still charge me for possessing a "look-alike drug." What I didn't know was that in the eyes of the law, the crime of selling a look-alike drug and selling the real thing were virtually synonymous.

After my scolding, he shut off his overhead lights and told us all to get out of there. We all knew that this was not a random event; I knew something about the stop was suspicious. The fact that he came up to the car, claiming to smell weed told me everything so we followed the officers at a distance and sure enough, they drove right to where I had told the prospective customer to meet us. It was then that I knew we had been ratted out.

The next morning, we drove to town at 6:30 and woke up the prospective customer at his bedside. When we had first arrived, we watched as he slept comfortably in his bed and then proceeded to "let him know" that his high jinks were not appreciated. The look on his face when we woke him up spoke volumes. We left there and went to the school to decompress. We needed to be seen by staff and other students in case an alibi was necessary. It wouldn't be iron-clad, but at least it would give a little resistance to any claims that were made by the kid who had called the police on us just the day before. After that morning, he never returned to school nor was he ever seen in town again. He and his mother moved away later that week. To this day, I have never seen him. Apparently, we must have made our point.

As I look back at my past, I sit here and shake my head. We weren't the worst kids to have ever lived in the world—there is always someone else who takes the cake—but we certainly weren't saints. Over the next few years, I continued to get worse. I had distanced myself from God and that meant that my life would only persist in its downward spiral.

Chapter 2

EXPANDING MY HORIZONS

I n the midst of all of my chaos, I realized that it was time for me to get a real job. I was 16 and needed some cash to pay for all of the things that a 16 year old thinks he needs. There was gas, cigarettes, alcohol, and weed to pay for. I needed some real money, and I needed it fast. In the past year I had worked as a dishwasher during the summer, but now that I had my license washing dishes wouldn't cover it. I weighed my options and decided to look for a job in a town called Lowell about ten miles from where I was living.

In no time at all I had developed a friendship with a fellow kid my age named TJ. Both of us were interested in getting a job so when the opportunity presented itself for the two of us to work at the same place, we submitted our applications. A day later, we received a phone call and were invited back for an interview. By week's end we were gainfully employed at the newest fast food restaurant in town.

Before the restaurant opened, they required us to go through orientation, and so we both went together. This was our opportunity to meet all of the people that we would be working with. Upon entering the restaurant, I was pleased to see that several co-workers were good-looking young women. I strutted in there, and, shockingly some of the ladies weren't exactly that receptive. I knew that all it would take is time and their attitudes would crumble. I was confident, cocky, and full of pride.

As I suspected, it took some time, but the girls lowered their guard, and we all began enjoying our time together. I was a huge flirt, and the girls didn't mind the attention. I took particular interest in one blonde girl named Brenda. She was pretty and had a beautiful smile. Our friendship grew and in time we developed a crush on each other.

However, just because my heart was softening for a girl didn't mean that it wasn't hardening in other ways. I kept a keen eye on the managers, and I noticed that several of them were stealing money from the tills. At the end of a shift, they would take all of the reports and scour over them, deleting various orders and tallying up the total. What they were doing didn't surprise me in the least. Truth be told, I had beat them to the punch and had started running my own scam.

My operation was quite simple. I would type the order up but not fully process it. It would show up on the back monitor, the back line would make the order, and I would give it to the customer like any other order. At the end of the night I would add up those orders and then remove that amount from the cash register. I was able to bring in a minimum of a hundred dollars every night without raising suspicion, and my drawer was never off.

Then one evening, I took a big step. I confronted one manager about the roll of money that he had just pocketed and told him that if he cut me in, I would keep his secret safe. He didn't even hesitate. He pulled out the roll and handed me a hundred. Each night we worked together, I would get some kick-back. That position became very lucrative, and to make things even better, my friend and I had begun selling weed on a daily basis so that we didn't have to pay for what we smoked.

As our criminal activities increased, we consciously did what we could to keep the business small, only selling about an ounce a day. There were other individuals who had been at it longer than we had, and we didn't have a steady supplier as it was. Had we stepped on their toes we would have shut off our only supply. However, what we intended to do and what happened were two different things. The longer I stayed in Lowell, the more people I met and the more people I knew, the larger my network became. During those days, there were a lot of people that came through my life, but I only considered a few of them to be real friends.

TJ, Brenda, and I had been working in the restaurant for about a year when the last of the managers that I had been extorting was fired. When he left, my easy money disappeared. Working at a fast food restaurant quickly lost its appeal. Once we had met the new manager we all began evaluating our choice of employment. Ultimately, TJ quit, and with that my options became increasingly clear.

I was tired of smelling like roast beef, curly fries, and turnovers. I thought that I would be better off just finding another local part time job. I had been bringing in pretty good money by selling weed anyway, so I submitted my resignation. By week's end, I already had a new position in my sights. My friend TJ had found work within a week of leaving and agreed to help me get employed if that was what I had wanted. I needed some extra income, so I asked him to put me in contact with his employer, and after applying, they hired me and placed us both at the same assignment.

T.J. had found work with a janitorial service and it was our job to clean a factory in town that made boat parts. Unbeknownst to me, this job would lead to incredible and everlasting changes in my life.

My first day with the janitorial service finally arrived, and I had no clue what to expect. I picked up TJ on the way and when we arrived there, we clocked in and walked back to our area in order to meet our supervisor.

As we walked down the hallway, I began assessing our surroundings. I could see who I was working with and it looked as though all of my co-workers were pretty decent. Our supervisor, whose name I'm not comfortable releasing, was an older man of Mexican descent. He was polite, yet authoritative. One thing that stood out was that his short stature did not detract from his commanding presence.

As we stood there listening to him give us our instructions, I couldn't help but notice that just behind his buttoned-up collar and just beyond the end of his sleeves were dark colored tattoos. My thoughts quickly returned to what was happening, and I did my best to concentrate on his instructions.

Once he finished telling us what was expected, he took each of us around to our prospective areas and showed us how to clean them properly. He was thorough and very particular about how we were to clean. After he left, TJ and I got to work. Even though I was hard-headed and disrespectful to most people that assumed to have authority over me, in retrospect, I think we both wanted to do our very best. There was something about our new supervisor that I liked, so I did what I could to earn his respect.

About two hours later, I met up with TJ and asked him if he wanted to go sneak in a joint during our break. I told him that I had found a closed-off portion of the factory that was empty and restricted to everyone, but was still accessible. He said that it was cool with him so I rolled a big joint, grabbed my smokes, and headed for the exit.

We had only taken a few puffs from both a cigarette and the joint when our supervisor entered the space barely 20 feet away from us. I had just taken a hit off the joint and my lungs were filled with smoke. I didn't have any idea what to do with either the joint or the smoke so I held the joint at my side and held the smoke in my lungs. My supervisor casually walked over and sat next to us. Then seconds later, he looked directly at me and asked if I was going to pass the joint or let it burn out.

Denying that I had it would have just been stupid since the smell was so strong. I exhaled and handed him the joint. He hit it a few times and then asked me if I could get rid of more of it. I hesitated and then told him that I could. I replied by telling him that I had an ounce in the car. He shook his head and repeated his question, "Can you get rid of more of this?" It was then that I realized that he wasn't asking to buy any, he was asking me to sell some for him. I hesitated to answer and then told him that I could. He stood up, looked at me, and as he turned to go back in, he told me to follow him home after work.

I didn't know what to think. Here I was, on the first day at my new job, and my supervisor was propositioning me to sell weed for him. At first I was afraid that he was trying to set me up, but the fact that he actually hit my joint basically convinced me that his offer was genuine. After work, as he climbed in his car, I climbed in mine and followed him home.

As we drove, I noticed that we were actually driving toward my house. I thought I had this guy pegged as being a city-dweller, but I was soon going to be shocked on many levels. When we drove past my house I was in disbelief. I had never seen this guy, yet it appeared as though he lived right down the road from me. All sorts of thoughts were going through my mind. As we continued driving, I decided to grab my knife and stun gun and tuck them away on my person. If this something was going to go down, someone was going to go down with me.

As he turned on his blinker, I realized then that I had driven past his house countless times before. I had several friends that lived within a half mile of him. Matter of fact, one of them lived right next door. Because of this, I decided to cover my face as best I could as I walked up to his side entrance.

He lived in a quaint little country house next to a lake. He invited me in and asked me to sit at his bar. I took a seat on the stool and watched as he walked into his bathroom. As I sat there, I looked around at the surroundings. Everything was spotless. The house's interior was beautiful. He had brand-new furniture that sat on newly installed tile and wood flooring. Minutes later he walked out of the bathroom carrying a duffle bag in his hand. He set it on top of the bar and then reached under the countertop and pulled out a triple-beam scale. Upon setting that on the countertop, he proceeded to open the bag and pulled out a ten-pound block of high quality commercial weed. The stuff was neon green. The only thing that made it commercial-grade is the fact that the 14 to 16-inch buds had been compressed.

He cut off and weighed up a pound, and then asked me how long it would take me to sell it. I assured him that it would take a day or two—I wanted to give myself some extra time just to make sure. He told me that I had a week, and that the price would be $600 for the pound. No matter how many I sold, the price would always be $600. I took my package and left. As soon as I got in the car, I called a friend. I explained to him that I had some mid-grade and that the price was $1400 for the pound. He affirmed that he was interested and told me to come on by.

I pulled into his driveway about 15 minutes later, and within a second of him setting eyes on it, the pound was sold. I called my new supplier and told him that I was ready for an additional one. It hadn't even been an hour since I left. I returned and picked up a two-pound block. After leaving his house the second time I placed a call to another friend and delivered those two pounds to him—I did all of this before the sun set. In a matter of one day, I went from being a low-level customer to being a mid-level supplier with an unlimited quantity of product and a very hungry clientele.

I continued working as a janitor in order to keep up appearances, but I was selling a lot of weed all over Kent and Ionia counties. The quality of my product was far superior to that of the competition—so much so, that the higher price did not affect my sales. The stuff was worth its weight in gold. It wasn't long, and I knew that my life would never be the same again. At one point, I even began ironing my stacks of cash at night in order to reduce the size of the bundle. It was then that I knew I was in business.

The cash and drugs were a natural attractant for trouble, and so I began arming myself. I had a couple of friends that I could trust that were as crazy as I was, so I began having them ride shotgun with me when I went on my runs. The guy that I trusted most was Bob. Bob wasn't just a hired gun; the guy was intelligent and knew what I was thinking before I said anything. The ability to communicate without speaking came in handy several times.

Bob's main job was to keep a look out for patrols, for rival dealers, and for any danger that might arise during a deal. If any of these circumstances occurred, he would have to deal with it appropriately. Depending on what type of day we were facing, whoever was riding shotgun was in reaching distance of any number of weapons, including a Remington pump 20-gauge shotgun with—let's just say—a smaller barrel. This shotgun however, was not loaded with birdshot, but with slugs and buckshot—each round alternating from one to the other. Bottom line, I was playing for keeps. I was dealing with large amounts of cash, and I was too small of a guy to be taking chances. So, I did what I had to—as do others who were in the same line of work.

A few weeks after I began operating at this increased scale, someone asked for 40 pounds. For an amount as large as that, I would simply add $200.00 to the price that I paid for each pound. That meant that when I sold my product, I would be picking up $32,000.00 at one meeting. This was the largest amount that I had moved up to that point, and since my normal supplier was out, I would have to go to someone that I was not accustomed to buying from. My nerves were raw. I had to pick up from an unfamiliar source in an unfamiliar location in Lansing, Michigan. I did not like dealing with individuals that I did not know.

Making things even more difficult was the fact that Bob couldn't go with me on this trip. Everything about this situation suggested that I should drop it and move on, but I had people with cash that needed a product and demand dictates the situation.

I called someone who I knew could handle himself, and I told him to bring a gun. We drove to Lansing, got off at exit six, and drove a few blocks to an alley that went behind a series of houses. We pulled up to our destination, got out of the car, and checked out our surroundings as we headed for the house.

When we walked up the steps the door opened, and we were ushered downstairs into the basement. There in the basement, were two African-American men holding AK-47's. They told us to strip. It was there that we had to leave our pistols. They allowed us to redress once they took the weapons and then to my surprise, a trap door in the floor opened, and we were ushered down yet a second flight of stairs. Never before had I seen a house with two basements.

We walked down into this second level, and there was a bar, a pool table, and another person stationed as security. It was there that we met the supplier. We were told to lay our money on the pool table in increments of one thousand dollars. So, I proceeded to lay out the $24,000 on the pool table. Once the amount was confirmed, the guard hit a button and from behind the bar, a conveyer belt started. In a matter of seconds, my 40-pounds of weed appeared. They handed it to me, allowed me to check it out, and once I saw that it was good, we bagged it into two large duffle bags and carried them up the levels until we got to the top. Once there, they gave us our pistols, and we left. Upon leaving, I looked at my friend and said, "Never again!"

Their operation was too one-sided. I knew that the next time, we probably wouldn't make it out alive. Many times an individual will allow one deal to go through successfully in order to lull you into a false sense of security, and then once the money is high enough, they'll flip the switch and take what they want. Unfortunately, that could mean the money, the drugs, *and* your life. If you're reading this from a prison or jail cell and you have any experience at this level in the game, you know exactly what I'm talking about.

On the way back, my friend told me about something that he had going on. He had a U-Haul truck full of "shrooms" (psychedelic mushrooms) coming in from Idaho later that afternoon. After seeing how much cash I was playing with, he knew that I had the network available to distribute his shipment.

He told me that he would sell each ounce to me for $80 and pound for $1000. Shrooms were a rarity, so I jumped on the opportunity. I met up with him later that night and looked at the product. I had never seen such nice shrooms. These were large "gold caps" with gold flakes in the stems. There were blue streaks flowing throughout both the stem and the bottom of the cap. Everything about these just screamed, "PROFIT!"

I sold these shrooms for $40 an eighth, which meant that I could make $257.50 profit from each ounce. Since I was purchasing them by the pound, I had the potential of making $4120 in profit per pound. However, most of the time, I stuck to purchasing them by the pound and selling them by the ounce. There were times that I would sell smaller amounts, but that was rare. I did my best to create an environment where the guys that dealt with me could make a decent profit themselves. I didn't want the price to go up too much. I wanted to maintain good prices while providing superior quality. That was my marketing strategy. I knew that if I provided quality at a good price, I would eventually surpass every competitor by selling not only larger amounts, but also by providing the best stuff on the streets.

My connections were incredible, and I did whatever I had to in order to protect them. The last thing either of us wanted was for their identity to be revealed. They were happy dealing with as few people as possible. It was by watching them that I realized that I needed to consolidate my operation. I needed to reduce the number of people that I dealt with. So, I spoke to several other successful dealers and agreed to begin supplying them while simultaneously passing my street-level contacts to them. Eventually, I was dealing with five to ten people a day instead of 20–30. It didn't mean I was any less busy, the guys that I had brought into the operation began making a lot more sales which meant that I had to continually restock their supply. Each day, I would drive an 80 to 90-mile circuit three to four times. Some days we didn't return home until 2:00 or 3:00 in the morning and by 9:00 a.m., the phone would start ringing again.

Looking back, I don't know how I found time to have a personal relationship, but I did. I always had a girlfriend that stayed close, and there was no shortage of women who wanted to hang out with us. When I reminisce, I can't believe that I put them in that kind of danger. Drugs, drug deals, and impaired driving were a normal part of my daily life. The car chases and bad deals were deadly, and there were moments when they were right in the middle of the mix. Anyone who truly understands all that love entails would never put their loved one at such risk; but in spite of believing that I was in love, I put those that stayed closest to me in a lot of danger.

Though I didn't realize it, my life was spinning out of control and the day would soon come where I wouldn't be able to handle the world that I had decided to live in. Funny thing is, had I known, it probably wouldn't have made any difference to me. I was past the point of caring.

Chapter 3

THE DAWN
OF A DARK DAY

Every day seemed to blend in with the rest. There was nothing to distinguish one day apart from the other, and I got to a point where I didn't know what day of the week it was. I remember a time where I couldn't even recall what month it was. From the time that I woke up to the time that I finally laid my head on the pillow, my life was consumed with selling drugs.

I had been on a non-stop schedule for weeks, and my current girlfriend was getting really annoyed. She had wanted to do some shopping for quite some time, but I hadn't had the time to take her. Today, I had decided that I would put my sales to the side and take her to Woodland shopping mall in Grand Rapids.

As we left town, I pulled out a bag of Hydro and began rolling a joint. Suddenly, I felt a sharp, burning sensation under my right shoulder blade. Not wanting to disappoint my girlfriend, I continued driving to the mall. All the while, I was doing my best to act as though nothing was wrong, but by the time we got there I was in no shape to go anywhere. I pulled the bankroll from my pocket, pulled a few hundred from the top and told her that I couldn't go in, that I would wait in the car until she got back.

Nearly 90 minutes later, I heard the door open, looked up, and realized that I had passed out from the pain. Though my girlfriend had never driven before, I told her to drive me home. She did as was asked and upon arriving home, I crawled into my bed. Two days later, my girlfriend called my brother and asked him to check on me. When I didn't answer my phone, my brother came to the house, kicked my door in, and found me collapsed on the floor. He raced me to the hospital in Ionia and called my family as the doctors began trying to figure out what was going on.

Hours passed. The doctors told my family that my pulse and breathing were normal, that they didn't know what was going on. My mom insisted that a chest x-ray be done. Upon getting the results, it was discovered that my right lung had been collapsed for three days—that was the sharp, burning sensation that I had felt.

My parents were extremely upset because the doctors had stated that my vital signs were normal. My mom knew that had they actually done the examination properly, they would have found the collapsed lung sooner. By the time it was realized, I had been in the hospital for hours. The doctors wanted to put a chest tube in immediately, but my parents feared their incompetence would complicate the situation even further. They decided to call an ambulance and have me transferred to Metropolitan Hospital in Grand Rapids.

About 20 minutes later, they were rolling my gurney into the emergency room. It was there that I saw a doctor approach me with a scalpel in hand. I asked him what he was doing, and he proceeded to inform me that he intended on putting the chest tube in while I was still conscious. I read off the staff's name tags and proceeded to threaten to kill them and their families if he even touched me with that scalpel. It was then that they decided that it would be best to put me under.

I awoke with a tube the size of a garden hose coming out from an incision between my ribs. With each breath, I could see the bright red blood coming out of my lung. It was then that they told me that I had nearly died.

For ten days, I sat in that hospital. Even though I had the chest tube I still wasn't out of the woods. Each day was a struggle. The pain was so incredibly high that they rigged a morphine drip that released the pain killer every half hour.

Occasionally friends would stop in. My friend Hope and her brother TJ came in to see me, only to have to step back into the hallway because of nausea. My complexion was ghostly, and they had never seen me so weak and vulnerable. Just the sight of me was enough to make someone nearly collapse. This collapsed lung had brought me to death's door, and I remained there for several more days.

Two weeks after my release from the hospital, I had a follow-up appointment with the surgeon who did the operation. He proceeded to inform me that I had six blebs on my lungs. Blebs are thin soft spots on the lung where the tissue is at risk for breaking. He told me that my lungs would surely collapse again—that it wasn't a matter of if, but when. He told me that when it happened again, that he could operate; but if it happened a third time, I would be out of luck.

I hadn't thought that by walking into the surgeon's office I would get a veritable death sentence, but that is what I saw it as. I decided right then and there that if I was going to die young, I was going to do so on my terms and not anyone else's. I was going to live life "pedal to the metal."

LIFE ON MY TERMS

After my lung collapsed, there seemed to be something missing. There was something about my life that just wasn't cutting it. I had money, girls, and everything else that comes with the game, but I wasn't happy. To top it off, not only was I frustrated with the doctor's prognosis, but I became increasingly frustrated with having to deal with the same product and the same people all of the time. A few weeks before my near-death experience, I had spent a weekend snorting coke. I had seen coke before, but I had never used it. This drug provided a completely different high, and the social circle surrounding its distribution was entirely different. Not to mention, the amount of money that could be made in my market was enticing.

Upon realizing that my life may not be as long as previously thought, I began seeing coke as a very real option for living life "pedal to the metal." I was faced with a challenge though; cocaine carries a big stigma throughout nearly every segment of society. The way I figured it though, I was already a drug dealer, so it didn't really matter about what anyone else thought.

After further contemplation, I decided to contact my primary supplier and ask him if "the family" was able to connect me with a steady supply of cocaine. As always, he didn't disappoint. The following day, he introduced me to my new coke supplier. He told me that I could front a minimum of 4 oz. of high-grade cocaine for $2200. He pulled out a sample so that I could test it, It was everything that he had said it was. I had heard of Peruvian flake, but I didn't think I would ever see it for myself. The layered iridescent pearl-white chunk was a sight to behold. I knew that like the weed they supplied, I would have the market. The quality was beyond anything I had ever seen. My competition wouldn't and didn't stand a chance.

As I began building new clientele, I made sure that I didn't forget my base. I still kept my weed sales going. Weed was my bread and butter. However, I knew that with the cocaine, my clientele would change drastically. The last thing I wanted was to start selling to a bunch of addicts, so I began looking for those who either only used occasionally, or those who didn't use at all. The problem was finding out who those people were. I had never been one to go to local parties. It just wasn't my scene. My perception of alcohol and the scene that surrounded its use had drastically changed over the last few years. I wasn't a fan of alcohol anymore, and I hated being around drunk people; but in order to find a secure circle of customers, I had to get out of my comfort zone.

On the weekends, I would show up to random parties with a backpack full of goodies and a friend carrying something to ensure that everything went as planned. I would let the host of the party know that I was there and offer him a deal on the merchandise. It didn't take long and people began catching onto what I was up to. It was really quite easy. There would be nothing but alcohol at the party, and then after I left, there would be a plethora of substances available. Though people didn't know my name, it got to the point that people would recognize me by my signature backpack.

The new product brought a completely different lifestyle with it. Nights of sleep were no longer part of my life. I began meeting people involved in the rave scene and started stepping into the underground circuit. Eventually, I met a man who would soon become a roommate. He was well-connected with the management of a production company that primarily dealt with artists making techno (electronic) music. It was at this time that I began experimenting with ecstasy.

Things were changing quickly. Instead of just weed, 'shrooms, and coke, now ecstasy, opium, and pharmaceuticals were part of my inventory. I began specializing in variety. I would have several varieties of every drug on me at any given time. I could provide the best of whatever drug you desired, and it was guaranteed to be top quality. Of course, not everything about my life was roses and sunshine. As my pockets grew, so did the danger—both internal and external.

Selling drugs isn't an easy occupation. My lifestyle was so strenuous that many of those closest to me would have to decompress after hanging for only a few days. After partying for four days, you could tell that it was time for a 48-hour nap and a good detox. There was a lot of pressure in my little world. If we weren't stressed-out by the feds and state agencies trying to close in on us, it would be because of our competitors. I couldn't even go on vacation without having rival dealers try to move in on my customer base.

One night, my friend and I decided that it was time to disappear for a while. I loved to go camping in the woods, so we packed up what we needed, picked up a couple of girls, and headed out into the country.

I had a spot that I liked camping in. There was an old country road that went back toward the campsite. The site was at the bottom of a valley. The only downside was that steep tree-covered hills surrounded the site. I didn't like being at the bottom of the valley, but at least we had cover. It was virtually impossible to get a direct line of sight on my position unless you were within the camps line of sight. To the north of our spot ran a stream that was too wide to cross without making noise, and the brush that surrounded my immediate area made it too difficult to creep up from any other direction without being heard.

After setting up the tent and getting the firewood, I tied Damian—my gator pit—up to a tree that rested in the middle of our site. Damian was a beast of a dog. He began training as a puppy, and by the time he was a year old, he was able to walk around the yard with a railroad tie connected to a body harness. This dog was nothing to be played with. One day, I tied him to the natural gas tank outside of my father's house, and by the time my father arrived home, the tank had been pulled from its foundation, and the gas line had been severed.

Damian and I became an awesome team. He had already proven to be a protector. Several months before, someone had tried carjacking me at a roadside store when Damian came across my lap and bit the guy's arm. I didn't even realize anyone was there until Damian had made the move.

My vacation had started off wonderfully. We had been having a great ol' time out in those woods. My friends cracked a couple cases of beer, and I brought out a drug that I had designed myself. The drug was called "Dealer's Choice." It contained cocaine, Molly (pure ecstasy), Valium, and OxyContin. I created it after not being satisfied with any of the effects of the ingredients when used alone.

By the time the sun went down, we were considerably high. It was nice to be away from the stress of my daily life, but my vacation was about to be rudely interrupted.

Around ten o'clock, Damian began growling in a low and steady growl. Until then, I had never seen him act that way. I knew something wasn't right, but I didn't know what it was. Not one to take chances, I told the girls to sit back near the tent while my friend and I got our guns. Even though I was camping, I wasn't going to go unarmed. We were both carrying Remington 20-gauge pumps with alternating buckshot and slug rounds, and I had a Marlin 22 magnum rifle with 17 rounds in the tube and one in the chamber. I also brought about a hundred rounds of ammunition—just in case.

As soon as we had the guns in hand, Damian began barking. He was pulling on his chain so hard that, at its center point, it was about six inches off the ground. That wouldn't be anything worth mentioning if it wasn't a tractor chain. This chain was really heavy, so for him to have it off the ground meant that he was intensely serious about getting whatever was lurking in the dark.

Our fire was burning brightly so it was nearly impossible to see anything beyond our campsite; and without any water, I couldn't put it out. We took position behind the trees, and I yelled out that whoever was out there had ten seconds to take off before lead started flying. About five seconds later, we opened fire.

Lead flew through the woods as fast as we could cycle the next round and pull the trigger. After I ran out, my friend opened up; as he was firing, I was reloading. After a couple of reloads, we stopped firing and let the smoke clear. One of the girls that was with us said she had heard someone scream. We turned our ears towards the drive that led to our campsite. We listened for any movement, and as suspected, we could hear some crashing in the woods.

I didn't want to escalate the situation, so I decided to stay in our position until morning. It was a long night and come sunrise, I was ready to go see what we had hit.

As we approached the drive, I noticed something completely out of place. There on the ground, was a broken taillight and a cracked cell-phone, neither of which had been there the day before. What I saw confirmed my suspicions. Someone had attempted to come at us. The interesting thing was that nobody—apart from those that were with me—even knew where we were. That meant that there was a mole in the camp. Someone that I had been sleeping next to was working for the enemy.

I sat back and assessed the situation. I had to figure this situation out before going back to camp. Whatever I did from here on out, I would have to do it carefully. After weighing my options I came up with a plan.

My friend and I walked back to the campsite and told the girls what we had found. They acted surprised, just as I knew they would. In return, I acted as though I didn't really care. I did everything like usual, with the exception of how I hid the stash that we had brought. I took a small portion of it and hid it while knowing that I was being observed.

As the day passed, we got high as usual, and I waited for the sun to go down again. I knew that something would happen tonight, but I didn't know what.

After passing out for a couple of hours I woke up and noticed that one of the girls was gone. I knew that she had left her friend holding the bag, so I didn't bother taking my rage out on her. I told my friend that I was going to go check out the crib and that he should stay at the camp with the girl who had been left behind.

I drove all the way home and found exactly what I had expected. Someone had kicked in the door, had ransacked the house, and had walked off with a measly quarter ounce of coke.

What I discovered is that the girl had called her ex-boyfriend and convinced him that she would be able to help him take my stash, and though it's true they did get seven grams of coke, they also got an enemy—an enemy who was calculating, unforgiving, and relentless.

I sat in my living room trying to decide what I should do. If I followed my heart, the day would end with me getting chased down in the woods by a state police helicopter and several Ionia County Sheriff's Department four-wheelers. That type of trouble was not justified by the loss of a mere seven grams. I decided to minimize the situation by calming the nerves of those involved.

I drove back to the camp and finished what we had started. We sat there for the rest of the week, occasionally going to town for food and supplies. For the most part, though, we went right back to having a good time. However, the day would come when those involved would drop their guard, and when they did, I would be there to get what was rightfully mine. Those who knew me best knew exactly how I would play it, and it wouldn't end well for those in my sights.

Chapter 4

AND DARKNESS DESCENDS

As I look back at my life, I am amazed at how crazy it was. I was either fearless or absolutely crazy. For years, people had been calling me "Crazy Greg" and "street pharmacist." Since I was imbalanced and usually had enough drugs to stock a pharmacy, I thought it was quite appropriate. The way I saw it, the crazier people saw me, the less likely they were to try to test me. I wasn't trying to be psychotic, I just was. My passive-aggressive behavior reached its max in the year 2000 when I felt that a few of my old "friends" in Lowell were not treating me with as much respect as I have would liked.

I had given a fellow dealer about $3000 to pick up five ounces of cocaine, and he only came back with four ounces. I knew how much he had paid because I had contacted the person that he had purchased it from.

After I received my four ounces, the offense just kept stewing in my mind, and I got angrier and angrier. I knew that he had pocketed nearly $700 of my money, and that was not acceptable. It wasn't the money, because $700 wasn't that much. It was the principle of the matter. When you have an agreement, you have an agreement.

After much contemplation, I decided to wait. My friend suggested that I let him make some money using what he had taken from the initial deal. I knew that he was a resourceful dealer so in time he would make a decent profit. It wasn't easy, but I waited. Three, then four, and then five months passed by, and after discovering that he was buying nearly double of what he had been,

I figured it was time to strike. I had waited long enough. It was time to shut him down.

I called a friend who was as fearless as I was and told him that I had a mission that I needed help with. I went and borrowed a truck from someone who lived 40 minutes away. Then I went to my house to finish preparing for the mission.

We waited at my house until 1:00 a.m. Since we were going to be hiding in the woods, I thought it was best if we held off on using any hard drugs. The last think I wanted was to start tripping out in the woods while staking out a job. We smoked some weed and made our final checks. We dressed in camouflage, applied face paint, and loaded the guns. When 2:00 a.m. arrived, we left for the target's house. We weren't sure what we were going to encounter, so I brought a little of everything. The individual we were coming up against was nobody to take lightly. He was as dangerous as a cornered cobra, and I knew it would be a mistake to underestimate him.

It was a quiet drive to his house. My friend and I were both trying to prepare mentally for the upcoming challenge. As we got closer to his house, the tension in the truck began ratcheting up. Our adrenaline was racing through our veins, and our hearts were pumping.

We drove past his driveway and took note of the neighbors in the area. Fortunately, he lived in a wooded area that had very few homes within sight of his driveway. We pulled over about a quarter of a mile from his house, hid the truck down a two-track road, and then walked through the woods to his property line. Once there, we settled in and waited for the sun to rise.

During the last week, I had watched the target closely. I had mapped out his work schedule, and I knew that he left every morning by 7:00 in order to be to work by 7:30. Waiting in the woods for him to leave for work was nerve wracking. In the past, whenever I had found myself in situations like this, my mind would race to the "what ifs." You try to be prepared for everything, but you never know what the other person will do if the plan that you are intending to execute does not go smoothly.

The night waned and daylight had just started shining overhead. Slowly but surely, beams of light began filtering through the trees around us. I knew that it wouldn't be long, and this situation would come to a head. My mind began to calm, and my thoughts focused. Again, the adrenaline began to pump and my senses heightened.

As 6:45 a.m. arrived, the front door opened, and the target exited the house. However, he wasn't alone. He was with a little English Terrier. I had never expected a dog, especially a little dog like this. We held our position, but were nervous that we would be detected. They walked down the driveway and came within 4 feet of our location.

As soon as we were directly across from each other, the dog began to bark. My hand tightly gripped the handle of the gun, just waiting for everything to crumble. Fortunately, in spite of the dog's actions, the target just kept walking. He pulled on the leash and told the dog to quit barking. Ever so slowly, the target moved out of sight. We waited a few minutes and watched as he and the dog made their way back to the house. This time, the dog walked right past our position without causing a ruckus.

My friend and I looked at each other, and I motioned to him that it would only be about ten minutes before the target would be leaving. As suspected, he exited the house at 7:00 a.m. and departed for work. When he drove past our location, I knew that we were going to succeed. He turned onto the road and slowly we rose from our hiding place and began walking across the lawn to the rear of the home.

I knew he had an alarm on the house, but I also knew that our location would make it difficult for the Kent County Sheriff's Department to respond any sooner than six minutes, and that was plenty of time to do what we needed to do. I had my partner go get the vehicle while I tried to find an easy way into the residence.

I wanted to make entrance in an area of the house where we could gain quick and unrestricted access to the safe that I knew he had owned. Thanks to some of the girls that he had kept company with, I knew right where the safe was, and I knew that it had not yet been bolted to the floor.

My partner arrived with the truck and positioned it for the ease of loading and departure. Now came the big moment, it was time to make our entrance.

With ball-peen hammer in hand, my partner approached the rear of the house and broke the glass to the back doors. As soon as we made entrance, the motion detectors activated the alarm. From that point on, we had 30 seconds to accomplish our goal. I wanted the majority of those six minutes to get out of the area, so we needed to act fast. The last thing I wanted was to be seen by the police on our drive out.

I ran through the living room to the target's bedroom. I made entrance into his room and saw the safe against the wall under a small table. My friend and

I looked at each other, knowing what we needed to do. Each of us picked up a side and lifted the safe from its position. Fortunately, the safe wasn't that heavy.

We put the safe in the rear of the truck and sped away from the scene. Once we had driven about 30 miles, we powered up our cell phones and began making calls as if it were any normal day. We went to Belding, a nearby town, and made ourselves known so that we would have an alibi in the area. Once I knew our presence had been noted, I decided to leave and go look at the score.

I drove down the dirt roads of Ionia County until I found a suitable location to open the safe. After about a half hour of driving, I finally located a place that I thought afforded both security and privacy. I opened the unlocked safe and counted the money that we had made. In total, we walked away with $6000 in cash, four ounces of cocaine, and nearly one hundred 80-milligram OxyContin pills. It was a lot more than the $700 that I had felt robbed of. But for me, what mattered the most wasn't the amount, but the principle. I knew this would send a message that would be heard loud and clear by all who lived and worked in the area.

We spent the rest of the morning offloading the spoils with the customers that didn't know the target. The last thing I wanted was the target getting any direct evidence as to who had done the dirty deed. The fact that he had an alarm on the house meant that the police would be involved in this investigation. It was imperative that I get rid of as much evidence as quickly as possible. The safe and its contents (apart from what I wanted) found their way into the swamps of Montcalm County. It was then that we decided to go to my house and get some rest. It had been a long day, and we both needed some sleep. I went to bed that afternoon feeling fully justified. Little did I know that this event was not over, nor would it be for nearly 12 years.

I slept well—so well, in fact, that I did not wake up until 8:00 the next morning. However, I didn't wake up to an alarm or a barking dog, but to the target standing in my bedroom doorway. He had convinced a roommate to let him in. She didn't have a clue what I had been up to the day before, so I couldn't blame her. Nonetheless, there we were—he was at the door, and I was in my bed.

He began voicing his suspicions, and as he spoke, he became increasingly angry. I could tell that this was not going to end peacefully, so I took the situation to a level that he never expected. I stood up, and in my hand was my favorite gun, a pump action Remington 20-gauge. I always slept with that next to me. Even when I had company I would keep the gun between the wall and mattress. Given the drugs and occupational stress, nightmares were a common occurrence, and though I knew that many of them were merely the product of stressors that I had encountered during my day, I didn't want to take a chance.

This morning, my paranoia paid off. The target didn't know what to think. One minute he had the element of surprise and he was in a dominant position, the next moment, he was running for his life.

Though months had passed between what he had done and what I had done in response, he still knew it was me. There weren't too many people willing to go head to head with this guy. He was aggressive, and a real fighter. The guy had heart, intelligence, and a bad temper—all were perfect elements for a volatile situation.

After I raised the gun, and he ran, I followed him out of the house. He scrambled to get to his truck and seconds later he was turning onto the street. As I walked back to the house, I began contemplating the situation that had just occurred. In organizing the mission I had assumed that eventually he would want to retaliate, but I also knew that he wasn't willing to risk as much as I was. I knew he still cared about whether or not he lived; I had no such cares. I took life one breath at a time. If the next one didn't come, then so be it.

As I began shutting the door, I turned back and looked at the sun rising above the trees. The beauty of the morning didn't escape me. However, I knew that in spite of the beautiful horizon laid out before me, the sun would soon set on this life I had so precariously built.

I had been riding this train for a long time. There had been a lot of stops along the way, but the end of the line was getting closer. Every once in a while, I could see glimmers of light shining through the windows of this speeding train, but for the most part, all I could see were shadows—the outline of life if you will. I knew that one day the ride would end. I had been around long enough to know that at the tracks' end sat a cliff so large and so deep that all that could be seen was a big black hole, a hole where darkness reigned.

Chapter 5

BRIEF GLIMPSES OF CLARITY

Somehow, I had gone from a young kid in church school to a drug trafficker. Not only was I trafficking drugs, but by now I was also a drug addict with an insatiable appetite for narcotics. I couldn't get enough, and it didn't matter what drug it was. Every once in awhile, brief glimpses of clarity would flood into my inebriated mind, but for the most part, the only things I thought about were drugs and money. One day while taking advantage of one such moment of clarity, I began reminiscing. My thoughts traveled to the last few years, and I realized that there had not been a single day where I had not gotten high — not a single sober day in over five years. I had been high for over 1825 consecutive days. I don't know how I did it. It wasn't something that I had planned; it just happened.

Years of using cocaine and ecstasy had taken a terrible toll on my body. After years of trafficking and drug abuse, I had developed such a high tolerance that even one foot long lines of cocaine didn't have much of an effect on me. I was frustrated with having to use so much. I voiced my concerns with an old friend from school. He told me that instead of snorting the drugs, I should just inject them. It was his opinion that I would use far less, and he insisted the high was much better.

My friend had been injecting cocaine for years, and despite being an addict, he had managed to keep his life together without anyone outside of his circle discovering his habit.

I knew that if I started shooting up, it wouldn't be considered acceptable, not even in my circle of friends. In order to maintain my customer base I knew that I couldn't go down that road, at least not yet. My business was already slipping, and I knew that if I let my addiction take me to that point, the situation I was facing would only get worse. For now I would just have to keep using at the elevated level that I was.

Later that same week, I began sensing the police closing in. Something just wasn't right. It's hard to explain, but my sixth-sense kicked in, and I became increasingly paranoid about doing any business. As I looked at the individuals around me, it became evident that everyone I was dealing with was heavily addicted to at least one substance in my product line—many were addicted to nearly all of them. It was difficult seeing so many broken people. Even I began to see my own brokenness; but seeing and acting are two different things.

I couldn't shake the feeling that I was being watched. I knew the police had been inquiring about me, and I also knew that they had tried getting people to set me up. Yet, of all the years I had been selling, this suspicion felt different—I knew they were getting close. Not wanting to get caught up in a sting, I decided that it was time to slow down my operation. I did more than slow it down, I brought it to a crawl, but that crawl wasn't slow enough.

I had reduced my customers to a handful of people that had been faithfully buying from me for years. I should have known better. The days after shutting down the main supply line were difficult for everybody. Those who had depended on me could no longer depend on me. Now, instead of dealing with someone they could trust, they were put in a position of buying from individuals who weren't so scrupulous. In spite of being crazy, I was known for having superior product and great prices, but I knew that the police were getting close, and the reliable money wasn't worth a lifetime in prison. If the police were going to have any chance of catching me, they would have to convince someone close to me to set me up—and that's exactly what they did.

About three weeks had passed, and the streets were drying up. My phone was ringing off the hook, and I ignored nearly every request for drugs—notice I said "nearly." What I didn't know was that someone I had been selling to for five years had been caught drinking and driving. Apparently he had been caught several times before, and the police told him that if he didn't do something drastic, they were going to send him to jail, and he was scared of doing time.

The Ionia County Sheriff's Department, in conjunction with the prosecutor's office, came to him with a deal. They said that if he would help them set me up, they would let him go. Of course it wasn't just me they wanted; they also wanted two other dealers close to me. The individual didn't hesitate to jump at the offer. He was released on bail later that morning, and the next day, he went to work.

I had never had a problem with this guy. He was a hard worker, and he always paid upfront, so I didn't suspect him—at least not immediately. One afternoon, I received a phone call from him. He asked if I would be willing to sell him seven grams of cocaine.

Though he normally bought three and a half grams, I didn't think anything was strange about his request. I told him that my car was in the body shop, and that I would need a ride to a local supplier's house. I didn't want to go through my usual source because he was extremely paranoid and would never sell to me if someone with me was a stranger to him.

I asked him to pick me up at 5:00 p.m. Prior to his arrival, I noticed a grey Chrysler driving by my house. The car didn't go by once, not twice, and but three times. Now, I lived out in the country, and out in the country, unfamiliar vehicles stand out like neon signs. However strong my suspicions, I chose to ignore the car and leave with my customer when he arrived.

Everything went fine. We arrived at the supplier's house; I picked up the coke, and went back to the vehicle. I handed him his cocaine, and we began heading back to my place. However, on the way back, as we neared one of the dirt roads that intersected with the road I lived on, I noticed that same grey Chrysler parked along the side. Immediately, I turned to the customer and asked him point blank, "Did you just set me up? I just saw an undercover parked on the side of Noddings Road!"

He tried to assure me that he had not set me up, and that the car was probably just a family member of one of my neighbors. Little did I know, our entire conversation was being recorded on a wire that had been placed within the dashboard of the truck.

He dropped me off at my home, and I went back inside. I was still suspicious, but nothing happened. No police came knocking on my door, nor was I pulled over during any day subsequent to this event. Since nothing had happened, I decided to hook him up two more times in the weeks to follow. The noose was tightening around my neck, and I didn't even know it.

Just over three weeks had passed since I had made the initial sale to my "old friend." A girl I had known for years was visiting, and we were doing what I always did: cocaine. Around 1:30 a.m. our supply ran out, and I made a phone call to a dealer that I knew in Saranac.

When he answered, I asked him if I could pick up a quarter ounce of coke from him. He said it wouldn't be a problem. All I had to do was go over and collect it. We hopped in my car and headed for town. As we pulled into the sleepy little village, I noticed two police cruisers sitting just off of the main road on a service drive. That wasn't uncommon, especially late at night. Usually they would sit there and talk with each other, trying to stay awake during their shift.

It was 2:15 a.m. when I arrived at my friend's house. I asked the girl with me to sit in the car, as I didn't expect to be long. As I walked up to the apartment, I noticed that things just didn't seem right. I walked down his hallway, and as I drew closer to his apartment I observed that his door was wide open.

Cautiously, I entered his apartment, went through the bedrooms, and realized that he wasn't even there. I decided to take off and call him from the road. I figured he might have had to meet a supplier real quick. Having to make surprise runs was nothing new. I gave him some slack and headed home.

As we drove out of town, I noticed that the cruisers were still sitting there. I drove north down a very familiar highway. This road had both large and small hills that continued for about five miles. After that, the road straightened out. As I got about two miles away from town, I noticed headlights in my rearview mirror. These weren't just any headlights; these were the headlights of a police cruiser. Years of seeing the headlights of police in my rearview trained me to be able to spot them from a long distance away. See, the headlights on a cruiser are brighter than the average car. I put the pedal to the floor and started looking for an exit. The girl thought I was crazy, but I knew that if I didn't react now, both of us would regret it.

We reached 120 mph, blowing through a stop sign at Potters road. I had grown up just a mile north of here. I knew that at the bottom of the next hill was my old driveway, a driveway lined with tall pine trees. My plan was to get there before the cruiser could catch up.

By now, I knew my friend was getting really scared. I crested the hill, and as soon as my taillights were hidden by the decent, I started slowing down. I was able to slow down just in time to turn into the driveway. I quickly turned the car around so that we were wedged between the trees with my front end facing the road. Not ten seconds later, a cruiser flew by the drive at about 130 mph. Fortunately he was going too fast to see us hidden in the shadows of those trees.

I watched as his headlights faded, and then I pulled out behind him, making certain not to turn on my lights. I drove about a mile north and turned down a dark dirt road that came out just south of my house. We made it to Johnson Road—the road I lived on. At the intersection, I looked around for headlights and then gunned it to my driveway. I hit the garage door remote making it inside the house just in time. As the light in the garage went out, a police cruiser drove by the house. Just then the phone rang. I noticed the number and picked it up. It was an old family friend. She just wanted to know if everything was OK. She had heard my name come over the scanner.

I assured her that she must have heard incorrectly because there was no reason for my name to be broadcast over the police frequency. It was then that I realized they were after me, and it was confirmed in the morning when I received news of what had happened to the dealer that I had gone to visit.

His girlfriend called me the next day and told me that after I had called, CMET (Central Michigan Enforcement Team) had hit his house. While I was in the apartment looking for him, the police were in the field that surrounded his apartment complex, chasing he and one of his associates. That night, he left the apartment with 14 grams of cocaine. When they finally caught him it was already gone. He had hidden it in the weeds as he was dodging their attempts to take him down. Ultimately, he punched one officer and was then taken down by several others.

Upon hearing this, I knew that it was only a matter of time, and they would be coming for me. He and I had many mutual customers, especially since I had just backed away from the game. My sixth sense told me to get my house in order because it would only be a matter of time, and I would be fighting for my freedom—fighting as I had never done before. My senses weren't wrong. The police waited three weeks and then made their move for me. They came "suited, booted, and ready for business."

Chapter 6

LIFE UNRAVELS

After my friend's arrest, I began tying up my loose ends. I knew that someone close had set him up, and I also knew that chances were good that they had set me up as well.

Just a week following my friend's arrest, another associate was taken into custody. He and his father were notorious for running guns and shipping weed up here from Chicago. Though we operated through a different network, we still recognized that our customer base was connected. When he was arrested, I knew that I needed to look for the common link between all of us. It didn't take long.

The individual that I had confronted just a few weeks back was a customer to all three of us. According to friends, in the last month he had purchased larger quantities than usual from each of us. I didn't need to hear any more. I began getting the word out. I wanted to make sure that nobody else was going to take the heat for the situation we were facing.

It was too late though. I hadn't put things together fast enough—none of us had. We had been too greedy and too trusting. All of us had already sold to him, thus sealing the deal.

As the days passed by, I began wondering when my day would come—I knew that it was coming and coming quickly. One day, I went home and asked myself, "If the police were to come in here, what wouldn't I want in my possession?" There was quite a bit of paraphernalia, but that was nothing (at least to me), but the semi-auto Russian SKS assault rifle in the corner of the room was a different story. The gun had a complicated past, and the history of how it and several other guns came into my possession was no less complicated. I decided it was time to get rid of as many guns as I possibly could—and fast. I couldn't take the chance of getting busted with them. Drugs + guns = time in a Federal prison.

I began making phone calls, and eventually I had distributed all of the firearms but one: the SKS. I didn't feel comfortable giving it to just anyone. This gun was a beast and was extremely dangerous if not kept in the hands of an experienced and responsible user. I'm not saying that I was exactly a responsible user, but I had grown up using firearms, and they felt like an extension of myself; but I knew that the same could not be said for everyone. I understood the power of a gun and knew that if not respected, it could be used to hurt the truly innocent, and in spite of being cold-hearted, I still didn't want that on my conscience—or what was left of it.

It had been several weeks since I had sold to the man that I suspected of setting me up. I woke up with a sense of foreboding. It was as if I could feel the walls closing in. I didn't want to believe it, but no matter what I did, I couldn't shake it. That afternoon a guy I knew called me for an 8-ball of coke (three and a half grams). I only had about six grams left, and I wanted to distance myself from anything that I couldn't get rid of immediately with a simple phone call.

I called him, told him to come over after he got off work, and then I called someone else from Grand Rapids that I thought might be interested in the SKS. I had been hesitant to part with it because it was the last gun in my possession; I wouldn't have anything left for my personal protection. However, the pressure to distance myself from all that could incriminate me was intensifying. The individual I called agreed on my price and said that he would be over around 6:00 p.m. And the gun? As long as it was "as described," it would no longer be in my possession by 6:15 that same evening.

The sun went down early that day. It was mid-winter and around 4:00 p.m. snow began falling and falling rather heavy. I checked the weather, and they reported near-blizzard conditions for the remainder of the night. I decided to hunker down for the evening. I saw no reason to leave. There had been many close calls on the roads that night, and the last thing I wanted was to be a casualty of ignorance. High speed chases down country highways weren't entirely unheard of in my world, and I didn't feel like wrapping my car around another tree.

As agreed, the customer stopped by after work and picked up his cocaine. Normally, I wouldn't allow a customer to use my mirror to cut up and snort coke, but with the roads being the way they were, I didn't want him to attempt to cut up and snort his purchase while driving down the road. As I look back at the situation, neither of the choices were intelligent, but it made sense then. While he was preparing to get high, the buyer from Grand Rapids showed up. I didn't really want to mix meetings, but I didn't have many options.

On this particular evening, I was at my father's house. I had been staying there for a few weeks while finding another place to live. One thing about my father's house was that I felt safe there. It was "home" for me. Locating a place to live wasn't as easy for me as it was others. I had to make sure that the residence was under someone else's name because mine would automatically raise red flags with the agencies that were investigating me.

The potential customer from Grand Rapids walked in, and I directed him to the room at the rear of the house. I showed him the SKS, its accessories, and features. He didn't even attempt to hassle with the price. He pulled out the money, paid for it, and left. The whole transaction from start to finish was over in less than three minutes. I watched out the window as he walked to the car and placed the rifle in his trunk. He got in, backed down the drive, and headed down the road.

Once his taillights were out of sight, I decided to join the other customer. I pulled out my personal bag of cocaine and made up a "foil." A foil was a particular way to prepare the cocaine. It allowed you to smoke it without turning it into crack. I smoked one foil and began to make another. This one though, had nearly one and a half grams on it. I sat there marveling at my handiwork. This was enough cocaine to get 15 people high, yet it was all mine. I look back at what used to impress me and shake my head. If only I knew then what I know now.

As I prepared to ignite the lighter, I heard something outside my window. It was then that I heard the pounding on the front door. The first thought that popped into my head was that someone was trying to get into my house and here I was with no gun.

The bangs became progressively more aggressive, but I knew I still had a few minutes. Robbers rarely knock before entering; I knew it had to be the police. I also knew that the door they were pounding on was only going to open if I allowed it to. I had reinforced it in two different ways. The only way it would open is if I removed the 4 x 4's that were bracing it against the base of the opposite wall. Somehow, I doubted anyone on their team was big enough to break that.

I wasn't ready to open the door. I decided that I would do this on my terms, as I did pretty much everything else. I looked out the window and figures dressed in black were swarming the exits, waiting to pounce. I looked at the guy who had just purchased from me, he was as green as Kermit the Frog. I tried not thinking any less of him, but couldn't help but laugh a little bit inside. Then they pounded on the door again and that inner chuckle disappeared. I knew I couldn't leave them out there too much longer—if not for my sake, then for theirs. It was a blizzard out there, and the last thing I wanted was to get tried for killing a cop.

I looked at the "foil" that I had just made and decided to take a few hits and then open the door. Several pulls later, I decided that it was time. I walked out of the room and headed down the hallway for the south entrance. As I neared the door I could hear the officers notifying the other police that someone was coming to the door.

I removed the brace, opened the door, and fell to the floor as fast as possible. I don't mind doing something under my own power, but being forced into a position by someone else is frustrating.

In seconds they were on top of me, putting me in wrist and ankle restraints. I watched as they cleared the house room by room. Minutes later, I looked across the floor, and there in front of me was the customer, but what I didn't think about was my father. He had been in the dining room and was rounded up in the sweep in the same fashion as the rest of us. Here was a man who had never before been in real trouble. He was bound, angry, and humiliated. The look I saw in his eyes that night cut to the bone. That look had more of an impact on me than anything that had come before it.

As I looked at the figures around me, I read the vests: DEA; CMET; WMET; Michigan State Police; Ionia County sheriff's department. Nearly every law enforcement agency operating openly in Michigan was represented, and they were all there for little old me.

It was awkward watching the police go through all of my belongings. It was as if there were a swarm of bees moving around me, each on a mission to gather something that would destroy my life.

After about 20 minutes, the police had confiscated several bags of evidence: a laptop computer, and several used bags that I had used for my drugs. There was still residue visible and I knew that no matter what I did, I was going to have a possession charge.

After several minutes had passed, they put all of us in a seated position and asked me if I would be willing to work with them. If I would, they would release me on the spot. If I wasn't willing to cooperate, they would take me to jail and charge me with three counts of "Distribution of Cocaine Less Than 50 Grams, Possession of Cocaine, Breaking and Entering with Intent," and a slew of misdemeanors. I looked at the customer as they offered him the same deal, and he took it. I figured he would. He was as scared as they come. I, on the other hand, told them to take me to jail, and that they did.

I was booked into the Ionia County jail on the charges they had promised and was placed in a holding cell that smelled of vomit until I could be arraigned by a judge in the morning. It was an interesting night. While sitting in the back of the cruiser, I had managed to stick ten Fentanyl patches onto my body. I was wearing an inordinately large sweatshirt when arrested and during the search, they didn't see the front pocket, the pocket that contained two boxes of 75 microgram Fentanyl patches. When brought into the jail, I was strip-searched, but the officer wasn't looking for clear transdermal patches stuck to my body. He was looking to see if a bag of cocaine fell from my armpit or from between my legs.

After an uneventful evening in a drunk tank, I awoke to one of the trustees placing a breakfast tray through the slot in my door. I stood up, took the tray, and began eating. Today would be the beginning of a new experience. This was an environment where I had virtually no control. For once in my life, someone else was guiding my movements. To say that I felt uncomfortable was an understatement.

I finished eating the two pieces of bread and small bowl of cereal and began looking around at my surroundings. On every side of me were other cells and in them were more inmates. I looked into each cell and took inventory of who was about to be placed into the general population. In the very last cell, I saw one of the individuals who had been picked up in the same sweep that I was caught in. I had already heard what charges he was facing. They included trafficking, home invasion, and sales of narcotics. Like myself, he was facing some serious time.

About 11:00 a.m., I noticed the officers taking him out of his cell. He was led into the area where the detectives' offices were located. As he passed my cell I banged on the glass. When he looked over I signaled for him to stay strong. He dropped his head and kept walking.

It took about three hours for the officers to bring him back to his cell. Three hours was far too long for a meeting. As he walked past, he continued without so much as even looking in my direction. It was then that I knew he was out to save his own skin and that it was everybody for himself. That put me into a very precarious position.

About 15 minutes later, three officers approached my cell, opened up the food port, and asked me to back up to the door, put my hands behind my back, and to stay still. I did as directed, and they placed handcuffs on me. Once out of the cell I was led into the same room that my old business acquaintance had just exited.

I walked into the interview room and noticed that across from me— on the opposite side of the table—was Detective McNinch. Officer McNinch was the lead detective for Ionia County's narcotics squad. He was also one of the primary detectives for a joint task force called CMET (Central Michigan Enforcement Team). This officer was well known for crossing the lines. His occasionally unethical actions made those who came across him leery of even talking with him.

He could sense that I was suspicious. He walked across the room and approached me. He asked the officers behind me to release my handcuffs. Hesitatingly, they did as asked. I wrung my wrists in order to ease the discomfort and noticed that the detective was holding his hand out as if to shake mine.

He said, "I really need to shake your hand." At first I thought he was being sarcastic, but he was sincere. I slowly raised my hand in order to shake his, still unsure of what he wanted. As he shook my hand, he said that it was a privilege to meet me in person. I was taken back by his statement. He continued by saying, "It has taken us over three years to get you, but we finally got you."

After the initial pleasantries, I sat down and asked him what it was he wanted. I knew I wasn't brought back there to make friends. He took a seat and opened a black leather-bound folder. Several pieces of paper were pulled out and slid across the table toward me. There, for the first of many times, I read a list of the charges that the police department had accumulated. I already knew what they had formally charged me with, what I didn't know was just how in-depth the case was.

Upon seeing the details, I called home and spoke with my mother. I told her that I needed a lawyer, and a good one at that. They had only charged me with the cases that they knew they could convict me on without any resistance. The rest were cases that were still being worked.

Informants were being utilized and files from various agencies were being compiled. I knew that if I didn't get out of there or make some sort of plea agreement, that it would only be a matter of time before the DEA would be sitting across from me.

I could've gotten depressed, crawled into a corner, and given up, but that wasn't my style. I knew who the police were using to get close to me, and I knew that the person they were using was someone with a severe drug addiction. I knew that chances were good that the person they were using was skimming from the same pond he was swimming in. What I mean by that is that it was likely that the informant was either stealing from the drugs being bought from me, or he were taking the money that was being used to purchase from me. A drug addict wouldn't give away a guaranteed fix. All the informant had to do to get high is use the situation to their advantage, and I was going to find a way to do the same with the situation I found myself in. If possible I was going to ruin the informant's credibility by bringing into question the authenticity of the purchases that he made. I was going to do whatever I could to minimize the impact of the blow that I was incurring.

In spite of all of the negative issues, I did have several good things going for me. By this time I was 22 years old, and even though I had been dealing for six years, I had no previous adult convictions, and in addition to that, I had the ongoing medical issues with my heart and lungs. Those things combined, I knew I had a reasonable chance of avoiding prison, but I knew jail time was definitely in store. And so, the arduous pre-trial process began.

For four months I was transferred back and forth between Kent and Ionia County correctional complexes. Ultimately, I had to hire two lawyers to handle my case because two different counties had active charges. I nervously awaited the outcome of the negotiations. Every once in a while, my lawyers would stop by the jail and fill me in on the progress, but the days of not knowing were getting to me. There was a lot of stress in the unknown. Finally the day came.

My Lawyer said that if I pled guilty to two counts of manufacturing cocaine less than 50 grams, that I would receive time served, $8000 in fines, court costs totaling about $2500, two years felony probation, intensive outpatient drug rehabilitation, and I had to pay back the money that was spent purchasing cocaine from me. In addition to that, I had to pay for the K-9 units involved in my arrest. The money just kept adding up, but I knew that was the cost of doing business. They even charged me for the days that I had been incarcerated.

The arresting officers were NOT HAPPY. They had spent years trying to get me, and here I was, strutting out of jail—and I hadn't even been formally convicted yet.

The day of my release actually came as a surprise. We were all locked down for the afternoon count when my name was called over the PA system. All I heard was: "Emelander, pack up your stuff. You're out of here!"

I didn't even know what to think. Was it possible? Are they actually going to let me out of here? I didn't wait for them to change their mind; I packed up my stuff and headed for the door.

As I left the jail, one of the officers told me that my dad was there in order to visit me. I walked around the jail to the visiting room, walked in, and sat down next to my father. He didn't even realize that it was me. It took him a few seconds before he noticed I was there. He looked at me and then began frantically looking around. I half wondered if he thought I had escaped. It wouldn't surprise me if he had; I definitely had it in me. It was then that I told him that I had been released.

Once I climbed into my father's car, I began looking over my release papers, and I realized that my lawyers had worked out a deal that I was to be released and then formally sentenced the following day.

The next morning, I went into court in Ionia, pled guilty to the two counts of distribution of cocaine and then headed for court in Kent County.

Seeing the judge in Kent County was more intense than it had been in Ionia. The Central Michigan Enforcement Team had been working for years to catch me, and to see me walk relatively unscathed really irritated everyone involved.

I remember walking into the courtroom and reading the plaque on the judge's bench: "Judge Robert Reford." When my case number was announced, I approached the bench, pled guilty, and then waited for the judge to execute the sentence.

The judge looked me in the eye and said, "If I ever see you again, I'm going to throw the book at you." I quietly backed away from the podium. I was just happy to finally be out of jail. Kent County added on some additional court fines, restitution, and then sentenced me in conjunction with what Ionia had handed down. I walked out of the courtroom without any additional jail time.

It would be easy to think that this was the end of the story, but the journey was far from over. In all reality, it had just began. Even though I had dealt with the criminal charges, I hadn't dealt with the reason that I had committed them.

In spite of the claims I had made in the courtroom, that I would never commit those crimes again and that I was remorseful for what I had done, the truth is that I was not any different than when I had walked in there. Sure, I was sorry, but I was simply sorry that I had been busted.

The months to follow would set the stage for events that would make what I had already been through mere child's play. The darkness that had enveloped me was now beginning to churn in the recesses of my heart. The decisions that I would make in the weeks to follow would determine the path that I would walk—a path of destruction, heartache, and turmoil.

Chapter 7

THE BATTLE BEGINS

Upon release I sat down and had a heart to heart discussion with my parents. It would be a long time before I was truly converted, but I believe that this was the start of the journey.

I had to admit that I could not continue to live in the circles that I had been grown accustomed to. My health, my safety, and my life were all in the balance. While in jail, I had gotten a glimpse of what awaited me if I didn't change my life. My motivation for change was merely superficial, though; I was motivated more out of fear for what could be than sorrow for what had been.

Day after day, I had seen the food trays come through the doors; I had seen the daily fights that went from the dayroom or shower to the cell. The blood spraying from the mirror to the bunk was a sight that wasn't quickly forgotten; yet that isn't what made the strongest impression. What impressed me the most was the loneliness. No matter how well a man tries to hide it, there is always a split moment when you can see beyond the walls that are built up. That moment is never more noticeable than when the mail arrives or someone is called out for a visit. The reaction or lack of it from not getting a letter or visit from a loved one says it all.

I didn't want any of it. I was tired of everything that incarceration was, and in all reality, I hadn't even *seen* incarceration yet. I was motivated from what I knew could be if true change didn't occur. I knew that this was a chance rarely experienced by individuals who had been where I was. Before me sat an opportunity to begin living in a whole new way. I could finally walk away from all of the things that I had felt trapped within—or so I thought.

In order to help facilitate the transition from the drug culture to a normal existence, I decided to move to a small area about 30 miles from where my base of operations had previously been. I figured that as long as I didn't contact anyone from my past, and as long as I stayed away from the type of lifestyle that I had been involved in, the chances of getting swept up in the whirlwind of my past would be lessened. Little did I realize that my problems had less to do with location or friends, and more to do with the problem resting deep within who I was and who I saw myself as.

I wanted a normal life, but I didn't really know what that meant. I had not lived a "normal" life in so long that I didn't have a clue how to obtain it. I had been living in the fast lane for so long that I didn't even know how to slow down. I decided not to sell drugs, but I hadn't made the same decision about using. I was still delusional enough to believe that I could control my addiction. I quit using hard narcotics like cocaine, but began using pharmaceuticals. I had access to Vicodin, Fentanyl (which is 80 times more powerful than morphine, milligram for milligram), Avinza (24-hour sustained-release morphine), and a handful of other opiates through a local pain clinic. I had legitimate injuries from my past, but I didn't have any type of real discomfort to justify the quantity of narcotics that I was receiving.

I began abusing the medication, and soon, I could tell that my tolerance was increasing. I could see the same thing happen with pharmaceuticals that had happened with cocaine and every other substance that I had used to get high. I could see that no matter what the substance was, I was going to continue to develop a tolerance and start chasing the high.

Within two weeks of being released, I had moved all of my belongings to a small place north of Sheridan, Michigan. My new home was nestled in the country next to a large lot of woods. The closest gas station was only about a mile away, so at least I had food, snacks, and alcohol within my grasp. Up until this time, I had never really been a drinker, but I really wanted to continue getting high. I had no intention of being sober, no matter what may come. I didn't care that I was on probation. I figured I could con my agent as I had done everyone else in my past.

I still didn't recognize the level of my addiction. I still saw myself as relatively sober. I would get drunk on a daily basis, but I didn't see myself as an alcoholic. I fulfilled my court ordered rehabilitation with flying colors and did it while high. I had no real sense of where I was going or what I was about to go through. Frankly, even had I known, I don't think it would have mattered. I had not yet hit my own personal "rock-bottom." I was in just as much trouble as I had been before—maybe more—because now I had a false sense of security, and that was extremely dangerous.

For six months I lived in the country, but the day came where I couldn't stand the isolation. Every day was the same: pop some pills, take a few drinks, and get high. I did this every day. Finally, I spoke to my parents and told them that I had decided to move to a town a few miles away, a town called Greenville.

Now, Greenville is nothing to write home about. It's but a small town located just inside Montcalm County. I saw it as an opportunity to mingle, to create new friendships, and hopefully, to figure out what I was going to do with my life. I was tired of living day-to-day with no goals or aspirations, and no apparent career opportunities.

I told those closest to me that this would be the opportunity that I would need in order to really get my life on track. I hadn't yet learned that it isn't the location that makes one truly successful, but the character that one possesses. In time, I would learn these valuable lessons, but it would take something much greater than what I had experienced to open up my eyes.

Eventually, I did move to Greenville, and as expected, nothing changed. My days were filled with the same activities. The only difference is that I was now doing them with others. The emptiness was still there. In spite of having girls around me all the time, the loneliness was still there. I wanted more, needed more, but had no clue on how to obtain it.

Greenville was a bust. After about a year I could see that nothing was going to change. So, I decided to move back to Lowell, Michigan—the area where I had been basing my operations.

Before making the final move, I began searching for a job. My mother introduced me to a new business owner named James Fegel. Now James was quite a sight. He stood about 6 ft. 3 in. tall, had wide shoulders, a huge build, and every bit of him was muscle. He was an intimidating sight to behold, yet, as I talked to him, I could sense that he had a heart for individuals like myself. I could see that he had a burden for those who wanted more from life but had not found a way to achieve it.

During the interview, I told James about my past, about my struggles, and about my desire for more. Afterward, he told me that though he had applicants that were more qualified to take the position, he knew I had the heart for it. As

I found out in due time, James would do this over and over with individuals who were struggling to get a foothold in life.

Days after our first introduction, James and I drove up to Boyne City for corporate training. James was the new owner of a franchised restaurant called B.C. Pizza. The company was a growing force within the restaurant business then, and I saw in this relationship an opportunity to go somewhere in life.

I managed James's initial restaurant for two years, but once again my addiction and inability to be responsible with my own life got in the way. James continuously tried to help me see the situation that I was walking into, but I ignored him and ultimately ended up resigning from my position there.

My prescription drug abuse had progressed so far that now I was no longer taking my medications orally. Somewhere along the line, I had started injecting the medicine from my Fentanyl patches. That wasn't all though; I had also begun adding cocaine to the solution as well. My life was unraveling at an incredible speed. My days were quickly coming to a close, and my funds were running out.

The day finally came when my checking account was empty. I had squandered away all of the money that I had accumulated over the years. Every dime was gone, but that didn't stop me from spending.

I knew that it would take the financial institutions a few days to catch up to the empty account so I began writing checks—a lot of checks. I would go to Kohl's, JCPenney, Meijer, and every other store and gas station that came across my path. I would buy gift cards knowing that I could spend them like cash. I would also purchase large dollar items from the department stores and then return them for a cash refund then termed a "corporate refund." I began scamming the system for everything that I could get, but I knew that my time was drawing closer. The police would be coming for me in only a few days, if not hours.

Then one morning, I heard the knock on the door. I looked out the peephole and there stood Officer Valentine of the Lowell Police Department. I knew that if I lied to him and told him that it was merely an accounting error, he would leave and research it before having a warrant issued. As I suspected, that is exactly what he did. When he left, I packed a small bag and deserted my apartment. I left my home and everything in it, knowing that I wouldn't be able to return.

As I drove out of town, my anxiety began to increase. Where would I go? How would I survive? Even worse, how would I be able to afford my habit?

These and a hundred other questions began circulating through my mind. I had to figure something out, and I had to figure it out now.

There were still a few people who owed me money, so they were first on my list to contact. One by one I heard the reasons why someone could not pay me. As I went from person to person I began getting upset. The anger coupled with the withdrawals was too much to maintain.

That night I crashed on an acquaintance's couch. The next morning I went to my doctor's office to pick up a new prescription. Every thirty days I had to go into the pain clinic in order to see my doctor, but when I went in there this time I was told that the doctors office was cutting me off from getting any further prescriptions. Someone had told them that I had been abusing my medications. There was no opportunity to wean off of them, their decision was final.

I left feeling completely devastated. My tolerance was so high that only the strongest opiates would suffice. As I walked back to my car I made my mind up; I knew exactly what I was going to have to do. I knew the police would be coming for me, and I knew that my addiction was bearing down on me. In my mind there was only one solution.

I got in my car, put it in drive, and headed for Rockford, a town 20 miles to the north of where I was at. As I drove towards Rockford I weighed the situation and tried to see if there was any other way to obtain the prescriptions that I needed. Every idea was met with an apparently insurmountable obstacle. By the time I snapped out of my thoughts, it was dark, and I was pulling down the drive of one of my friend's mother's home. I had spoken to her in the past about my issues with medication. Like me, she too had prescriptions of morphine and other opiates, but unlike me, she didn't abuse her medications. She had a morphine pump installed within a small area on her body. This provided a steady stream of medication so she didn't need to take the pills that her doctor had prescribed. My plan was to see if she would be wiling to sell me the medication that she had accumulated, but as I pulled up, I saw that her husband was home. I knew he would be suspicious of me, so I simply left a note on the door and asked her to call me.

My phone never rang, and after several hours my body began screaming for its fix. So once again, in the cover of night, I drove up to Rockford. As I pulled into the drive, it looked like her husband was gone, but I wasn't positive, so as I approached the door I rang the doorbell and knocked on the door, but nobody answered.

Frustrated, I decided to just go in. If she was home, she might not have heard me knocking. I walked in and saw that all but the kitchen lights were off. It was then that I decided to just take the bottles of morphine that were sitting on the counter. I walked over, put them in my pocket, turned, and walked out of the door.

Chapter 8

A FUTURE FORETOLD

The ride back to Lowell from Rockford was filled with mixed emotions. A part of me was filled with happiness because I had just scored about 600 morphine pills, but another part of me was filled with regret and shame for what I had just done.

I drove over to another friend's house and began preparing the drugs for injection. I handed my friends a few but kept the majority for myself. It was my hope that the pills that I had just scored would somehow last awhile, but it was only a matter of days, and I was once again trying to figure out where my next fix was going to come from.

I quickly realized that I was in trouble. Not only were my thoughts filled with fear about going through withdrawals, but once again, I couldn't escape the feeling that my time was coming. Warrants had been issued, and the police were looking for me. I hadn't even attempted to cover my tracks as I had in the past; because of that, the police were able to quickly put things together. A big part of me was tired of fighting; just tired of being tired. To make things even worse, thanks to the warrants, my ability to travel was seriously impeded.

It felt as though the walls were closing in on me again, so I decided that it would be best if I didn't stay at one place longer than a day or two. I knew that I had enemies out there that would jump at the chance to get me out of the way.

From this point on, my days were filled with traveling the back roads of Ionia and Kent County. My daily goal was to stay out of sight and to find a place to lay my head at night. The most difficult part was that this was all occurring during the middle of winter. There were nights when I couldn't find a suitable place to stay, so I had to sleep in my car. On one night in particular,

I remember parking in an orchard so that passing traffic wouldn't see my car. I crawled into the backseat and pulled some blankets over me. However, in the middle of the night, I woke up shivering and covered in sweat. The withdrawals, combined with the cold temperatures, had sent me into a state of hypothermia. I nearly froze to death that night, and I knew it. Death was at my doorstep, and it began looking more and more inviting. What did I really have to look forward to? My family was scared to deal with me; my friends were afraid to have any contact with me; what was left? What did I have left to live for?

That morning, I made a decision that I would live the rest of my life regretting. I decided that when the time was right, I would break into my own mother's house in order to steal her medication, just as I had done to my friend's mother. Never had I imagined that I would ever do something like this to someone that I loved, but there I was, breaking into my mother's house. By the time that I had made it to this point, nobody was safe. I had crossed that invisible line that every criminal knows exists—that unwritten code of conduct. Breaking into your own mother's house was something that even societies worst criminals have refused to do, but I was prepared to do just that.

So much had happened in such a short span of time. In a week that was already filled with so much sorrow, I was informed that my friend Brent had died in an apparent drug overdose. I knew that he was depressed and that he had even attempted to kill himself earlier in the week, but circumstances surrounding this event were different. Something didn't seem right.

The story was that he had stolen $600 from a car that he had broken into. He then bought some heroin from a dealer we knew. Those that had been with him at the house that day said that he went into a back bedroom to shoot up once he had gotten the dope and hadn't been seen after doing so. They said that after a couple of hours they suspected something had happened. When they went to see what was up, he was found dead. He had injected the heroin, fell to his knees, and there he died.

The owners of the house then called the dealer and told him that he had to come take care of the body. The dealer showed up, and with their help, loaded his body into the trunk of his car. From there, they drove to the hospital where they pulled Brent's body from the back of the car and dropped him at the hospital's emergency entrance. They said nothing to the staff; they just got back into the car and drove away.

It would be a couple of months before I found out that he had most likely not taken his own life. It was rumored that he had been given a "hot shot" so as to remove him from an ongoing investigation into a dealer of ours. Brent was on parole, and in spite of repeatedly violating that parole, he never went to prison. The dealer suspected that he was working with the police, so in order to alleviate his concerns, it was rumored that the dealer simply gave Brent a loaded dose of heroin.

However, at the time of death, I thought that Brent had killed himself to end the struggles that he was facing. The similarity of our situations wasn't lost on me. Both he and I were running from the consequences of the decisions that we had made, and neither of us saw a constructive solution to the issues that we were facing. It was with these events on my mind that I decided to break into my own mother's house.

And so, I drove to Saranac and pulled over into a gas station parking lot. I got out and called her house from a payphone to make sure that nobody was home. When the call went unanswered, I drove to her home, walked up to the door, and smashed the glass window with a hammer that had been in my trunk. I reached in through the glass and unlocked the door.

As I walked into the once pristine house, the alarm went off. The siren began blaring in my ears, but even louder than that was a voice screaming, "What are you doing?!" However, both the alarm and that voice from within were drowned out by my desire for opiates. My heart pounded as I grabbed the medications and ran for the car. My mother's home was just outside of town so I knew the Sheriff's deputies response-time to the alarm was going to be anywhere between three and ten minutes. I had only been in the house for 15 seconds before I was back in my car. I raced down the driveway, merged onto the roadway, and then took the back roads all the way to a friend's house in Lowell.

It's amazing how every time I had drugs, I had friends, but once the drugs were gone, so were they. I wasn't under any false sense of who I was around. I knew that those around me were not true friends, but fellow addicts who, like myself, were struggling to stay "right." It was amazing how far I had strayed. Never had I thought that I would do something so despicable to the person who gave me life, the person who had raised me from a baby, the person who loved me unconditionally.

Once the numbing effects of the drugs wore off, the shame slowly settled in. The weight that I was carrying only grew with time. I could distract myself for a moment, but I couldn't escape the magnitude of the pain that I had caused. Though my heart had grown cold, there was still a spot of warmth for my mom. Unfortunately, the pangs of addiction were louder than the love that I had for my own mother. Addiction is a detestable thing.

One morning, about four days after I had stolen her medication, I called my mom and tried to apologize to her. I could hear both pain, hurt, and fear in her voice. I was no longer the son that she had raised. I was someone else entirely, and I knew it just as well as she did. I could tell that what I had done, had finally made her come to a point to where she had to let go. She could no longer advise me or support me. The decisions being made had to be mine and mine alone. When we hung up, I knew that it would be a long time before I would be able to speak to my mother, if ever again.

In the weeks that I had been on the run, I had crossed lines that I had never even approached before. I had dealt drugs, done drugs, tried to take people out, robbed drug dealers, been in high speed chases with police, but I had never broken the unspoken rules that exist in every family. Once I reached that point, there was no turning back. Nobody was safe. If I could steal the medications that my mother needed, there was nobody that I wouldn't hesitate to take on. I had actually reached a point of desperation that made me extremely dangerous. I had no care for anyone anymore—not even myself. I was actually so disgusted with myself that I was ready to have it all end. How could I continue living in the same space with the people that I had done so many bad things to? Thoughts of suicide were a daily occurrence, but I wasn't there just yet.

The nights were as cold as the days were empty. I had heard that the police had been raiding homes in search of me. They rightly suspected me of committing home invasions in multiple counties. They wanted to get me off of the street before someone got seriously hurt.

The cops were getting close, so I decided to park my car in a friend's garage. Their house had already been searched, so I thought that it would be a safer place to lay low.

The day after parking my car at my friend's house, I realized that my car keys were missing. When I came back to the house I was told that I had to get my car out of there. The police had returned suspecting that I had been there.

Fortunately, the windows on the garage were all covered, so they couldn't see it parked just feet from where they were standing.

I didn't want my friend or her children to get in trouble for helping me out, so I called Brenda. It had been over a year since we had last spoken, but I knew that she had an extra set of keys to my car. It was midnight when I made the call, and true to the friend that she was, around 1:00 a.m., she and her boyfriend Josh pulled in with some keys to my car.

I didn't tell Brenda what I was really facing. She knew something was up, but she didn't know the extent of the trouble that I was in. As Brenda and Josh pulled away, I started my car and got ready to drive out into the cold night.

As I left the housing development where I had been hiding, a heavy depression began falling upon me. The shame, the doubt, the self-hate began welling up within me. As I drove down the road I pulled into the driveway of someone that owed me money. I knew he wasn't home, so I parked my car in his barn and broke into his house so that I wouldn't freeze to death. This would be my last night of freedom for years to come.

As the sun rose on February 7, 2005, I decided that today I would end it all. I was tired of living on the run. I hated who I had become, and I saw no hope for the future. What could be left for someone like me, someone who had done so much wrong to those who were closest to me?

I pulled out of that driveway and headed to my father's house. I knew that he had a pistol that I could gain access to. Fifteen minutes later, I crept up his driveway and scoped out the scene. Once I saw that he was indeed gone, I walked around to the back of his house and smashed out a window on the lower level. I cleared the glass out of the way and made entry into the house. I ran up the stairs to where the gun was stored.

I knew that he would suspect me. Nobody else would have known where the gun was, but at this point, I didn't care. My future was bleak to say the least. I stole both his gun and some money that I had found within the house. At best, my plan would result in me getting enough prescriptions to not only get high, but enough to finish the job that I didn't have the guts to do.

My plan was to rob a pharmacy that I had scoped out in the past. I knew where the Fentanyl and OxyContin were locked up, and I knew where the key to that lock was stored. The head pharmacist kept the keys on a chain around his neck. All I had to do was get those keys, gain entry into the safe, and my problems as I saw them, would end one way or another. I figured that even if the police interrupted my plan, I would commit suicide by cop. I had had enough.

As I left my father's house, I called a friend up and informed him that I would be coming through town. I told him that I was on my way to go "hit a lick," that it would result in us getting a lot of dope. Little did he know that I had already made my mind up, that if it came down to it, I was prepared to take someone's life. I was tired, tired of running, tired of being a drug addict, tired of being hated by everyone that knew me. I had lost all love for those around me. I felt as if the world had given up on me, and I had given up on it.

I drove through Lowell and picked up my friend in the parking lot of a local restaurant. He got in, and we sped away without uttering a word. The entire ride out of town was quiet. He looked down and saw the 40-caliber Ruger pistol wedged between the front seats. After glancing at me, he picked it up, slid the slide back in order to cycle a round, and saw that it was loaded and ready for business. He looked at me with a quizzical look, but didn't say anything. He could tell that today was going to be a day that neither of us would forget. Like me, he too was in a state of hopelessness. We were both drug addicts with no home, no apparent future, and no foreseeable hope. I had given up on life, and I knew that what we were about to do next was going to alter the course of not only our future, but also the futures of those who got in our way.

We had been driving for about ten minutes. We were approximately 11 miles from Lowell, and only 15 minutes from our destination. I crested a large, steep-sloping hill on M-21 outside of Ada. As I began descending on the other side, I saw a glimmer of white on a driveway off to my right. Glancing over my shoulder I saw that it was a Kent County Sherriff's car quickly pulling onto M-21. He was coming, and he was coming fast. There was no doubt in my mind what he was planning on doing. I knew he was coming for us so I gunned it. I floored the gas pedal and sped up to 85 miles per hour.

Before I had driven 100 yards, I saw yet another cruiser coming toward me from the west. I quickly switched into the left lane and slammed on the brakes so that I could make the turn onto Spaulding Avenue. As I made the corner, I noticed yet another cruiser headed toward me. It was then that I realized that my day had come. There was nowhere else to run. Even if I outran one car, the chances of me getting beyond three were nearly impossible. I had contemplated suicide many times in recent days. Death by cop would be an easy way to do it, but I wasn't going to go alone. If I was going to die, then so were these cops.

A Future Foretold

I surprised everyone by quickly turning into a parking lot and slamming on the brakes. The police were right behind me. As my car came to a halt, they boxed me in. I quickly unhooked my seat belt and reached for the gun. I had decided that I was going to end the misery, once and for all.

Chapter 9

THE GAVEL DROPPED

As I reached over, the gun was gone! I looked up and my friend was triggering the gun's clip release. The ammunition clip fell out from the handle. I screamed, "Give me the gun!" He responded only by cycling out the chambered round and throwing the gun under his seat. Right then, I looked to my left and saw one officer with a gun pointed at me, while another opened up my door and told me to put my hands above my head.

The officers descended upon us like locust on a wheat field. As the officer pressed me up against the car, a state trooper pulled into the parking lot. I could tell that this arrest was going to make their day.

They searched me and placed me in the back of one of the cruisers. As he set me into the back, one of the other officers screamed, "GUN!" I looked up and saw my friend, now co-defendant, in handcuffs on the pavement. The officers, with gun in hand, looked up with a pale white expression. I leaned over and looked at the officer who had pulled me from the car. He, like the others, was in a little bit of shock. They had run up on my vehicle without doing a proper felony stop. What he didn't realize was how close he had come to being shot. The full realization of the situation settled in when one of the officers approached the car that I was in. The officer rolled down his window, and the approaching officer said, "That gun was fully loaded with cop killers."

The scene was surreal. Never had I imagined that they would have gotten me without me doing something fatalistic. The thought of death was so ingrained in my thoughts of the future that I never really imagined the possibility of something other than death.

While sitting in the back of the police car, a sense of peace came over me.

It was actually quite unexplainable. The anxiety of what would be was gone, at least for the moment. I took a deep breath and asked the officer, "So, why did you pull me over?"

He replied, "Well, for a lot of reasons, but mainly this one." He lifted up a wanted poster with my name and picture on it. He said, "These were handed out at roll call this morning. You made the most wanted list."

The Greater Grand Rapid's news agencies would all go on to run stories of my apprehension. I was convicted in the court of public opinion, and I knew that after that response, I would be facing some serious time in prison, but my mind wasn't focused there. Upon entering the Kent County Correctional Facility, I was logged into the database, placed in a holding cell, and given a paper-bag lunch. Once I was placed in the holding cell, I pulled my coat over my head and fell asleep.

For weeks I had been on the run. Sleep was never restful, but that day I slept with a depth that I haven't since experienced. I woke up nine hours later by a jail officer. I was told that I would be going to D-1, a larger holding unit. There, I would await my arraignments.

I sat in D-1 for five days. Day after day, I went before judges from various counties via video court. I will never forget the reactions of the inmates and officers in the room as the judges read off their list of charges. I don't believe the inmates had ever seen a skinny white guy get charged with as many crimes as I had been. After five days, the charges were complete. I was facing about 29 felonies and countless misdemeanors. The dates were scheduled for me to face five different judges in five different courtrooms. An additional county chose to drop its charges once they saw the numerous charges from the other counties.

From D-1 I was sent to the medium security portion of the jail. As the barred gates slid open, I was handed a blanket. I knew that yet another journey had started. I walked the length of the dark hallway, listening to the sounds of the other prisoners locked within the jail's steel walls. Each cell housed eight men, eight men who were filled with anger, anxiety, and anticipation of what was to come.

As I approached the last cell, the officers activated the door's release. I opened it and walked into what would be my home for the next few months.

I had never been in this section of the jail. It was clear from just a casual glance that this section was old—really old. There were six metal bunks and two plastic coffin-shaped pieces measuring eight inches upon which two more men slept. Apparently, this was Kent County's solution to the problem of overcrowding. In the center of the rear wall was a toilet. There was nothing separating the toilet from the rest of the cell. Those who used it were in full view of everyone else. I knew that jail was degrading, but this brings it to a whole new level.

I looked at each person one by one. As I moved my gaze to the last person I was surprised. I actually knew the guy—his name was G.

G was a beast. Though he was only about 5 feet 10 inches tall, the guy had biceps about as big as my waist, and I am not exaggerating. G loved to work out, and his workout included a push-up routine on his fingertips with his arms fully extended.

G and I had first met in Grand Rapids on Oakdale Avenue. For months, I had been down on the O.A.K., providing promethazine with codeine, morphine, and mid-grade weed. In exchange, I received large amounts of crack cocaine. G was an O.G. (original gangster) in that area, and because of my dealings on the streets of Grand Rapids, we had made each other's acquaintance.

As he stood up from his last set of push-ups, he looked up and smiled. His gold teeth shone, and his grin said it all. He was glad to see someone he knew, as was I. It was a real comfort to see a familiar face in a strange land. I made up my bunk, took inventory of everything in my surroundings, and laid down to sleep.

For the next four and a half months, sleep would be my best friend. Aside from reading, there was nothing to do. The cells were kept so cold that you didn't want to be out of your bunk. Remember, when I came into the jail, it was the beginning of February. I still recall one day when all of the heaters broke down—we prisoners were literally freezing. For one whole day, we sat under our blankets, trying to stay warm. Later that evening, the officers shocked us by coming by in the night with two extra blankets for every inmate. That should give you an idea of how cold it was. Had it not been desperately frigid, they never would have considered such a thing. Many of us spent the night awake under our blankets just praying for the heater to get fixed. It would be two more days before that relic of a heater was repaired.

When I was awake, I would read novels. Sometimes, I would read a novel a day. Every week, the library cart would come by so that I could renew my selection. It had been a long time since I had read anything besides a *Physicians'*

Desk Reference or *The Pill Book*. It was here that my appreciation for the written word was restored. Every day, my interest in study was further cultivated. My perspective of what was and what could be was broadened, and for once in my recent life, I could see a glimmer of the "old Greg."

Every week in jail taught me that although incarcerated life is not pleasant, it is still life. There is still value in living even though it may not be the life that I wanted to live.

Occasionally, I would be called out for an appearance before a judge. There was nothing pleasant about those experiences. They perpetually reminded me of what I had done. Three months into my incarceration, I was totally sober. That was both comforting and unsettling. I was comforted because I saw that sobriety was possible, but I was haunted by what I had done while high. Though I was locked away from the world, I was not locked away from the memories of what I had done to those who actually loved me. There was a constant river of pain that ran through me, and to some degree, that pain still exists today.

After four and a half months, the week had finally arrived. This was the week that I would be sentenced. My lawyers arrived at the jail to discuss the plea agreement. They told me that the prosecutor had offered me a deal of 20 to 30 years in prison. That meant that I would serve a minimum of 20 years and a maximum of 30. That seemed too long, even for what I had done. I was actually upset because someone in my cell had shot somebody and only received seven years for manslaughter. Yet, here I was facing a sentence equal to a life term in most states. I instructed my attorneys to reject the deal. I told them that I would rather waste the courts time and money in a jury trial than to take a deal like that. They returned that afternoon with a deal that, though pleasant, was still hard to accept. The new deal would have me serving a minimum of four years and a maximum of 15. I took it.

One week from that afternoon, I found myself in the courtroom of Honorable Judge Robert Redford. I stood behind the podium, short of breath and filled with anxiety. The judge walked out of his chambers and took a seat at the bench. He called the case file and asked for the lawyers to proceed. The prosecutor stood up and read the terms of the plea agreement. After the prosecutor finished speaking, the judge asked me if I understood the plea agreement and then finished by asking if I had anything to say.

I stood up, addressed the court, and told him that I was genuinely sorry for the damages that I had caused, both within my family and abroad. I didn't pour my heart out or offer any tearful plea. I knew that there was nothing to do that would affect the outcome. Once I pled guilty the court adjourned and scheduled a day, one week later, that I would be sentenced.

The day finally arrived when everything was going to finally come to a head. The jail transported me to the courtroom, and within 30 minutes I was, once again, standing before the Honorable Judge Robert Redford. The pre-sentence proceedings were still fresh in his mind. He had looked over my case files thoroughly and was not impressed in the least. As the proceedings continued, he looked directly into my eyes and told me that I had been a menace to our community. He continued by telling me that even though he would accept my plea of "guilty," he would not accept the plea agreement that the prosecutor and my lawyer had worked out.

Looking at me he said, "Mr. Emelander, the last time I saw you I told you that if I ever saw you again, I would throw the book at you, and that is exactly what I am going to do. I have re-scored your sentencing guidelines according to the crimes that you have committed, and in accordance with that I now sentence you to the Michigan Department of Corrections to serve a term no shorter than 84 months and no longer than 240 months."

And then, the gavel dropped.

Chapter 10

THE LAND OF THE FORGOTTEN

t was only a matter of hours before I was on a transport van headed for the Michigan Department of Correction's Reception and Guidance Center. That is a flowery name for what we all called "Quarantine."

The Michigan Department of Corrections (MDOC) was the proud owner of the world's largest walled prison. Originally opened in 1839, the State Prison of Southern Michigan, at one time, housed 6000 prisoners. Today it is carved up into four facilities, only three of which remain open at the time that I am writing this book.

After about a 90-minute ride, the transport van pulled onto a road that was near the prison. Once the 20 foot razor wire fences appeared, it was like they never stopped. Eventually, we pulled up to a series of gates and were given entrance into the RGC (Reception and Guidance Center).

The van doors opened, and one by one we prisoners were allowed to step out. I did my best to maneuver in the cramped space, but the hand and ankle cuffs made it difficult. What made it even worse was the fact that I not only had wrist and ankle restraints, but my ankles and wrists were both connected to a belly chain. This chain was then connected to the prisoners in front of and behind me.

We walked through a series of gates and doors until we came up to a building. Once given access to the doors, we walked in and were greeted by a row of tables behind which were several officers. The transport team handed the officers the property that we had brought from the county jail. Everything except our legal paperwork was thrown away. We were not allowed to bring anything into the prison except our legal documents. This wasn't particularly frustrating for me since I didn't have anything, but as I glanced back I did see one prisoner getting rather upset because his Bible, a Bible that had clearly been a gift, was thrown away with absolutely no regard. There was no offer to mail it home, or make it available for someone to pick it up. It was tossed out like any piece of trash. Now, at this time I was not religious in the least, but something about it struck a nerve within.

We were then all taken to a room surrounded by huge glass walls. In the middle of the wall was a pile of jumpsuits and next to that, a small pile of flip-flops. We all stood there, kind of confused; then the officer told us to take off all of our clothes. It was obvious that this was the place where the county jail uniforms would be exchanged for the "state blues."

When men tried to retain their dignity by keeping their underwear on, they were intimidated and told that everything had to come off. There were kids there that had just turned 18 that were extremely timid about undressing and rightly so. We were told that nothing was allowed in the prison that did not originate there. And so, we did as was instructed. I took off all of my jail-issued clothes and put on a prison-issued jumpsuit.

If that wasn't bad enough, we were all directed over to a bay of open air showers and told to strip, shower, lather, and rinse. Everyone had to shower before going any further.

Now showering is one thing, but located directly across from the showers was another room made of glass walls filled with a bunch of other men, and by looking at these men it was clear that some of them saw this as a great opportunity to get a free peep show.

I knew that this was part of the process. Deep inside, I knew that in the grand scheme of things this was nothing compared to what I would yet face. I was smart enough to do as instructed and move onto the next step. I could see the fear beginning to well up in some of the men. The looks in their eyes said everything. Others sat there attempting to appear indifferent, but that was just as revealing as was the fear.

Admittedly, this is when I began asking myself some serious questions. Up until now, I had been rolling with the punches, just going through the motions. But now—now I was really beginning to wonder what the rest of my life was going to be like. So far, things were not looking too good. As I looked around I was not exactly inspired.

It wasn't long before I realized that much of prison consisted of doing nothing but hurrying up in order to wait. The officers had us going from one department to another. First it was registration, then orientation, and finally we went off to the quartermaster where we were outfitted with three sets of clothing, bedding, pajamas, and shoes. Honestly, after only having two pairs of jail clothes for five months, receiving my prison uniform was kind of like Christmas; but no amount of clothes could take away from the environment that I had to wear them in.

The whole day was spent in this building. We had HIV and HEP-C training followed by testing. The instructors made it very clear that there were infected people all around us, and that within the prison environment, the surfaces would have bodily fluids on them that could transmit said diseases if contact with an open wound was made. We were given instructions on how to clean our cells and how to clean the sinks, toilets, and showers that we would use. However, what they didn't tell us is that the "chemicals" that we had access to were too weak to kill the weakest germ let alone one of the most deadly viruses known to mankind. What I would find out later is that the cleaning solution provided required a long "dwell time" in order to have *any* range of effectiveness. Now tell me, who is going to wait 20 minutes to use a toilet when it is a "public" toilet? Clearly the solution was there for looks and nothing else.

Finally we had been to all of the initial stations. The time came for us to go to our housing units. Up until now none of us had had an opportunity to look at the housing units. Finally, as they gave us our bunk assignments, we were able to look at where we would be laying our heads. As we walked out of the main admissions building, there in front of us was a massive building the length of about four football fields and about six stories high. What we saw in front of us was merely one of five sections. The building was fashioned like a hexagon. Tall walls of razor wire separated each of the sections so that the next section could not have access to the ones beside it. Each of these walls had multiple layers, and each of these layers were lined with high voltage electrical fences. Then, at the corners, high above the fences rose the gun towers.

If the buildings weren't intimidating enough, the sight of all of the razor wire was. However, the fences and buildings weren't the only thing that sent a message. Between the fences and the road sat a series of gravestones clearly visible to all. The message, whether intentional or not, was clear. Within the MDOC, life is very fragile.

As I sat there, I was filled with an odd new realization. I felt the threat of death come, not from the prisoners that surrounded me, but from the institution that held me captive. As I began looking at the men around me, I saw a threat that faced the incarcerated, a threat that many overlooked. The threat of death was real, and the evidence was everywhere. All around me were walking corpses. Men who, though alive, had died long ago. Though they were breathing and could speak, they were as dead as anyone buried in the graves that bordered the fences of that prison yard.

The officer led me and several other men across the yard to our housing unit. Though the distance to the unit was only about 150 yards from the intake building, it seemed as though it took a lifetime to reach. As we approached the entrance, I began looking at those walking next to me. To my surprise, there next to me stood a woman, at least I thought it was a woman. I looked to my right and asked the guy next to me, "This place isn't co-ed, is it?" He just looked to my left and laughed. It was then that I realized that the person going into the unit with me was a transvestite. This place just got more bizarre with every step. I had truly entered the twilight zone.

We stepped inside the unit, and as I stepped forward, my eyes were immediately drawn upward. The interior of this massive building was lined with cells encased in cast-iron bars. There were cells stacked about six stories high, and they stretched over a hundred yards in length before finally reaching a wall that separated my unit from the next.

The housing unit officer called us over and told us where each of us would be "bunked." My cell was located in the center of the building, four stories in the air. I walked up the stairway, lugging my duffle bag of property until finally reaching my floor. As I turned the corner to walk down the hallway, I realized that the only thing preventing me from falling over the edge of the walkway was a one-and-a-half inch wide pipe whose height was barely above my thigh. This pipe ran the length of the hallway and was supposed to act as the safety rail. Clearly, it was only there for appearances because it served no real purpose except to provide a false sense of security.

Within about a minute, I reached what would be my new home, and it was then that I realized how much I missed the comfort of my own bed. Here, sitting before me sat a metal bed with a steel plate for a box spring. The mattress was a lumpy plastic-covered mass measuring three inches thick on the end and three quarters of an inch thick in the center, I could tell that any sleep I could manage to get would be anything but sound.

I settled in by unpacking the clothes that I had been given and by making up my bed. At least tonight I would sleep on clean sheets. Having slept in my car while on the run I could now appreciate the bed and bedding that I had. Once finished, though, I realized that there was nothing left to do. Here I was, completely alone with absolutely nothing to occupy my time. There was nothing to do but think.

For the first hour, I was able to occupy my mind by trying to plan out everything that I would do the next day, but I was always faced with the reality that no matter what I planned, I had absolutely no control over whether or not I was able to accomplish it. After the first hour had passed I found myself staring out of the bars in order to see if anyone else had found something worth doing, but as I looked at those within my line of sight I could see, that like me, they were all "twiddling their thumbs."

Though I was bored now, I knew that the boredom was only momentary. I knew that it wouldn't be long and I would be praying for the boredom that I now experienced. With this realization, I laid down and closed my eyes. As I laid there, question after question ran through my mind.

It wouldn't be long, and I would be facing the largest challenge of my life. Up to this date, nothing in my life had been as important to my survival as the step that I was about to take. The choice that I would make would reverberate not only through the Michigan Department of Corrections, but also throughout the lives of everyone that came in contact with me. This was going to be the most important decision of my life.

Chapter 11

MEMORIES, MIRACLES, AND THE MASTER

The days began to imperceptibly pass by. It was difficult to know what day of the week it was, and I had only been in the Michigan Department of Corrections for about two weeks. True, I had been in the county jails for five months, but they were nothing compared to prison. Over the past two weeks I had gotten a good chance to examine the characters of those who were imprisoned around me. The individual to my left had caught his wife in bed with another man and used an axe to unleash his anger. The person to the right was imprisoned for multiple counts of rape. The stories were all different, but the result was all the same. Here we were, all in the same prison, all facing the same punishment. I couldn't escape the fact that in society's eyes we were all the same; we were all unfit to be in society. The words of my sentencing judge reverberated throughout my mind. I had truly become a "menace to society."

When the words "menace to society" were first spoken, the weight of what they meant didn't really bare upon me. But as the days passed by in that lonely cell, I began thinking about what that really meant. I had every opportunity to be successful. I had good parents who loved me, who supported and believed in me. I was intelligent and resourceful. There was no reason why I couldn't have achieved any profession that I chose to pursue, yet here I was in prison. Where did that young Christian boy go, the boy who used to read all of the time and memorize pages of poetry? Where was the young man who loved his family and felt loved by his family? I had become a monster, someone who, in spite of all of these things, could look at those who loved him without seeing their love.

I could do to my family what I had done to everyone else. There was very little "me" left inside, and yet I could feel something stirring within.

That afternoon as I sat there contemplating, it struck me just how numb I had become. I was practically emotionless. Coldness ran through my veins. Even today, nearly ten years after this time in my life, I find myself still recognizing a chill within myself. I spoke to one of the guys that I had befriended in the previous days, and he told me that the apathy—the numbness—was a byproduct of using drugs for so long, but I knew from years with Christ that it was also caused by rejecting the pleas of the Holy Spirit. When I had felt convicted for committing the wrongs against others, I ignored it and moved on. Not listening to those promptings from within had, over the ears, desensitized me.

After thinking about it, I could see how that would make sense. I had used cocaine for years, and for over a year, I had used ecstasy heavily in combination with several other drugs. Ecstasy was known for causing a person to go into a state of emotional numbness. After partying all weekend, many of us knew that we would experience several days of depression. They even gave it a name, "Suicide Tuesday," because many people were known to have tried to commit suicide days after using the drug over the weekend.

I knew that the numbness that I felt within was twofold. First, it was caused by all of the pharmaceuticals and narcotics that I had pumped into my body. Second, I believe the numbness was caused from my unwillingness to face who I had become and what I had done in order to become this person. You can look at my picture today, and what you will see is someone who looks like they belong in a library or classroom, but who I was then is not who I am today. Many men try to look tough. They try to look intimidating, but that wasn't my style. I didn't have to "look" like anything. Simply put, I was a little crazy, and I didn't care. For those who were with me on some of the "missions" that I put together, they *know*. I'm sure at some time one of them will read this book and recall the lengths that I was willing to go to in order to get the job done.

Here I was, sitting in a prison cell face to face with who I had become. There were no more drugs to numb my mind, no more distractions to pull me away from myself. I had to finally face the person that I had created, and I had to combine that with the fact that I still had nearly a decade (or more) to remain in prison.

The weight upon me was getting increasingly heavier, and, like any guy who is faced with a problem, I tried to find a solution. In an attempt to relieve my mind I decided to take a nap, but sleep evaded me. Hours passed by, and all I could think about was who I was, but then slowly my thoughts began to shift and a series of incidents came to mind.

With drugs came drug use and a lot of it. There had been times when my friends would overdose, and we would have to go to extensive measures to bring them back to life. Today, only one of those individuals is still breathing— my friend Bob. The rest have all died from suicide, overdose, or suspicious deaths. But on this afternoon, it was not them that continually kept circulating through my mind, it was me.

There were many days when everyone would leave my home to go detox, and I would be left to myself. There I was with a pile of cocaine and nobody to have to share it with, so naturally, I did what every other drug addict would do; I began using. Well, after having been high all day, my body was already overloaded with cocaine so the natural response is an overdose. Typically, your body responds by sending you into cardiac arrest. I was no different.

As I laid there in my prison cell, memories of overdosing came back to mind. I can remember the times when I would take a hit, collapse on the floor, and begin going into seizures. I would flop around on the floor like a fish out of water. You would think that this would be enough for me to re-evaluate what I was doing, but I would simply get back up and continue using. At times I would go back into convulsions.

I quickly realized that with all of the overdoses that I had been through, at the very best, I should be a vegetable, but here I was, perfectly healthy. Matter of fact, after two weeks of mental and physical tests, I could say that there were no visible or perceptible effects from the drugs that I had done. Had it not been for me telling the doctors about my previous use, they never would have known. That struck me as odd and made me more than curious. As I sat on my bunk, memories like this continued coming back to mind, memories of the times when my life had been spared during robberies, and then one particular memory came back to mind with astounding clarity.

One summer night, I had been at a house party out in the country. I had drunk a couple of beers (which was odd for me), and I had also eaten the gel out of two Fentanyl patches. I knew that my high would only increase, so I decided to leave around 2:00 a.m. I climbed into my car, and since it was closer than my place, I began driving the three miles to my dad's house.

I had only made it a mile when I came up to a sharp curve in the road. The curve had a really steep bank that went to the right. As I approached the point where my car would have to take the inside corner, a truck came from the other direction—and it was in my lane. I had no choice, I had to take the left lane, but that was virtually impossible to do successfully. All I remember was my car flying off of the road directly toward a tree line.

My car came to rest about 25 yards into the woods. Trees on both sides had crumpled my front quarter panels and doors, successfully slowing my vehicle down. Then I hit an oak tree with the front of my car. Fortunately, I had always made a habit of wearing my seatbelt, because as the car came to a halt, I could feel my body rise from my seat, only to be restricted by the seatbelt that crossed over my body.

I was somehow able to free my car, and within those woods was a small access road that the owner had built that went back to the main road. When the situation occurred, the miracle was never revealed to me, but as I sat there in that cell, my eyes were opened. The question popped into my mind, "What ever happened to the tree line?"

Bordering the woods at the roadside was a very thick line of trees. These trees had been there for decades and were not small saplings. These trees presented a formidable wall, a wall that I had never come into contact with, but why? My car left the road at a fast speed and at an angle. Had there even been a space large enough for my car to make it through at the initial edge of the road? How is it that I didn't make contact with any of the trees between there and the place where my car did stop?

The day after my accident I called the police to file an accident report so that my insurance would cover it. I remember him looking at the accident scene and saying, "I don't understand." I knew the officer fairly well, and he never elaborated on what he meant, but that day in the cell it dawned on me. He didn't understand how I never hit the trees that were standing directly in front of us. My brake marks went directly toward trees that were never hit, and my impact marks were on trees behind the ones I missed.

Of all of the things that I thought about that afternoon, that one memory affected me the most because I knew that what had happened was physically impossible. I had driven down that road hundreds of times, and I knew its layout like the back of my own hand. Even today, nearly ten years later, I can remember exactly what that roadway and its surroundings look like.

The question of "How?" slowly transitioned into "Why?" Why was I spared in that manner? I had done a hundred and one things deserving of death that normally would have resulted in death, yet I was still breathing. But why? Why was I still here? Sure, I was in prison, but I was still alive!

In Romans chapter two, there is a verse that says, "The goodness of God leads you to repentance." That day, reminiscing in my prison cell, I was face to face with the goodness of God. I was confronted with my wretchedness in the light of His love. What kind of a God loves someone like me enough to save his life when every part of that life is in rebellion to Him? Over and over that question kept circulating through my mind. What kind of God would save someone like me? Slowly the answer appeared. The kind of God who would saved me is a God who loves me, a God who truly loves me.

Chapter 12

I BEGAN BY HUMBLY SAYING, "FATHER..."

It had been a long time since the subject of God had crossed my mind. Even though I was raised a Christian, I had managed to leave every part of that experience in my past. However, on this particular day, all of that was abruptly brought back into focus.

With those memories fresh in my mind, I was now facing the revelation that not only was there a God, but there was a God who actually cared about *me*.

For years I had believed that the world centered around me, yet somehow the idea that God would be focusing His love and attention upon me just seemed too difficult for me to wrap my mind around.

I tried to explain away the events where my life had been spared, but the more I attempted to find natural reasons for their occurrence, the more convinced I became that something much larger was at play. I just couldn't shake the sense that I had been spared for a reason, but why?

As I tried figuring out what the answers were, a sense of remorse began to fill my heart. If God did have a purpose for me then that meant my parents were right. My whole life, my parents had told me that God had something special in store for me. As an infant, my parents had taken part in a dedication ceremony in which my life was formally dedicated to the service of God. I blew that off and chalked it up to one of those things that religious parents do. But what if God had really taken that to heart? What if all along, He had a plan to use me, and I had just been ignoring it? Even worse, had I ruined my opportunity to actually fulfill what God had wanted to use me for?

Every now and then, I would shake myself away from this line of thinking. I would try to convince myself that I was just exaggerating, that the boredom was getting to me, but that sense of being loved and desired never left. It was as if, once I had made it to that point, God was going to drive it home.

Memories of going to church as a kid began flooding back. Those were some of the happiest days of my life. Going to school in a place where I was actually cared for allowed me to grow both academically and spiritually. I missed feeling like that, feeling like I mattered.

It had been years since I had gone to school, but there, in that cell, I felt exactly like I had when I was younger. I actually felt like I mattered.

Occasionally, I would look out of my cell and be reminded of where I was. I was so lost in thought that my surroundings seemed to vanish. This was the first time that I had actually been "free" in a long time. Sure, I was incarcerated, but inside I felt as though I was free; I was beginning to sense the possibility of true hope.

The numbness that had dominated me for so long began to fade into the background. For the first time in over a decade I began sensing things, things that I had forgotten existed. So many emotions began welling up inside that I became overwhelmed; I didn't know how to process them. With the hope of a future came the recognition of what I had done in my past. It was like an anchor holding me where I was. The weight of who I was and what I had done prevented me from truly embracing the idea that I could never be anything other than what I already was.

How many of us are filled with shame and guilt? How many of us are so filled to the brim that we never move forward from those events? I cannot go anywhere in life without seeing individuals who appear as though their pasts are an ever-present reality.

As I sat on my bunk contemplating my situation, I came to the realization that in order to move forward I would have to deal with what I had done in my past. It had to be dealt with in such a way that it would lose all power over me.

For years I had been ignoring the inner voices of condemnation, but that didn't silence them. Though I had drowned them out, I still knew they were there. The drugs, the alcohol, the empty relationships—none of them could take away the inner turmoil that stirred within.

I knew what I had to do, but it was something that up until then I would have never actually considered. Deep inside though I knew that it was the only thing that would work. I needed peace in my life, I needed forgiveness, I needed hope, I needed to know that God was going to be there to help me through what I knew I would undoubtedly face, but there was only one way to have that assurance. I needed to submit, I needed to give up control over my life, my dreams, and give my daily actions to the One who really loved me. I needed to give my heart back to God.

Looking back at the years between my youth and adulthood, I can say that I was fighting against authority in all of its forms. I did not want to submit to anyone or anything that was not of my own design. I wanted to be in control of my life and my destiny. But that day, what I realized was that in spite of all of my efforts, I had never been in control of anything. I had been giving control over to someone who only had my destruction in mind. There was only one thing I would ever have true power over, and that was my ability to make choices, and with those choices came the consequences. Everything beyond that point was affected by variables outside of my control.

Before me was another one of those choices. The outcome and consequences were unknown, but what I did know was that all of the decisions that I had made by myself for myself had ended in destruction and chaos. Now I had a choice to change my whole life. I knew that if I dedicated my life to following through on the choice before me that it would mean that I would have to fight battles that were harder than any battle that I had ever fought. I knew it was a decision that would have a very large impact on what would happen in the days, weeks, months, and years to follow. So, I considered my options.

The options that I considered were these.

Option 1

Facing seven years in prison would present challenges that I had never encountered in my past. Prison was an environment where I did not have "home field advantage." I was young, white, and vulnerable. For someone like myself, there were generally only three choices that people thought were possible.

- You either fought (with the likelihood that you were almost always going to lose since nobody fights fair anymore).
- You gave in and became someone's bunk buddy and allowed them to fight your battles.

- You locked-up and asked the prison for protection in which they would promptly put you in solitary confinement once you told on those that were harassing you. Then, 30 days later they would release you onto the same yard with the same people that you incriminated.

None of those seemed like viable options for me. I had a strong urge to get a shank and gut the first guy that came at me, but then I knew that that would prevent me from ever getting released. It would only prove to strengthen the opinions that society had formed about me. It was tempting, but the consequences far outweighed the benefits. The other two possibilities were not options at all.

Option 2
This option was the most radical. Frankly anyone even embracing it would be considered by others in his/her position to be certifiably insane. The option is this, to…
- Give up all control and allow God to take care of you.

It seems overly simple while at the same time extremely complicated. Submitting one's life to something and someone who isn't physically tangible would be considered to be the result of insanity. However, as I looked at my life, the evidence of just such a power was overwhelmingly present.

People who truly knew me in my past will admit that it is a miracle that I am alive. I'm not referring to the type of thing where someone would consider me "lucky" but truly the result of something miraculous. The quantity of drugs consumed alone is enough to place me in that category, but the drugs were only one element in a very lengthy story.

As I sat there looking at option number two, I knew that it was useless to try and play out what would happen in my future. Trusting God meant that no matter what came my way, I couldn't respond or react as I had in the past. "Doing me" some would say, is exactly what got me to where I was at. Had it not been for some divine intervention, I never would have made it that far.

I have often thought about asking my co-defendant what was going through his mind the day that we had been arrested. What motivated him to take my gun, release the clip, remove the chambered round, and throw it under his seat? It wasn't just fear. Generally he wasn't the type to really care. I honestly believe that God had to have been speaking to his heart because he had taken that pistol and begun the process before I had even thought about reaching for the gun.

It was little things like that—things that were anything but "little" that really struck a nerve with me and motivated me to consider option number two.

The sun began to set, and day gave way to night. As the last few glimmers of light faded, I could feel the voice within begin to get louder and louder. I knew that today's entire experience was simply God calling me back to him. I knew that He wanted me to give my heart, my life, and my future back into His hands. It was like a father calling a son back home. I had been out all day and now that darkness had descended and the streetlight was on, my Father wanted me to come home.

There was a real battle going on inside. Every part of my being told me to ignore what I had revealed. I knew that my decisions would be far easier to make if I continued living as I had been, but I knew the consequences would result in me never having a future, never having hope, and never experiencing true happiness. I didn't know what giving my heart to God would really result in, but if I wasn't going to have happiness, hope, or a future apart from Him, what did I have to lose? Really, what did I have to lose? And with that, the answer was clear.

For the first time since I was a young child I knelt down beside by bed. I rested my head inside my palms, and I began by humbly saying, "...Father."

Chapter 13

BEGINNING ANEW

Hours seemed to have passed by. Exhaustion had set in before I rose up from kneeling over my bed. Originally, it began as a confession; by the time I finished, it had morphed into me pleading for His help. Somewhere between the two points, I had sensed my own helplessness. A glimpse of reality paired with a sense of the enormity of my situation weighed upon me, placing a burden within my heart. The more I prayed, the clearer God's love for me became, and the clearer God's love became, the more sinful my life appeared. Tears flowed as I poured my heart out to God. These were not tears of fear, but of genuine sorrow for the destruction left in the wake of my lifestyle.

As my conversation with God continued, the weight—not only of what I had done, but of what was yet to occur—became too much for me to bear. I knew that I couldn't cope with things the way they were. For years, I had "managed" by doing drugs, drinking, or any number of other things. However, that was no longer an option. Here I was completely vulnerable and ignorant to how I was going to get through the war zone that lay before me.

During one half of this prayer, I was conversing with God, the other half was spent talking with myself. Periodically my mind would start going through the "what ifs" only to come to the realization that the "what ifs" didn't really matter. I couldn't control anything in here. The only thing that mattered anymore is how I conducted myself. Manipulation had never produced any truly positive long-lasting results. Since manipulation wasn't an option and since I couldn't overtly control what happened in my environment, I was left in a situation where I actually had to exercise this foreign concept called "trust."

Slowly but surely I began wrapping my mind around the idea that I would have to trust in Someone (God) that I couldn't physically hear, see, or feel. Every bone in my body contradicted this new mindset that I found myself in, but the memory of God stepping in to save and comfort me superseded all of the "logic and reason" that presented itself.

Hours had passed, and my body ached as it never had before. All of my muscles, drained of their strength, could barely assist me as I rose from my position and rolled onto the bunk. I painfully leaned down and pulled the wool blanket lying at the end of my feet up over my chest.

I lied back onto my pillow and took a deep breath. As I exhaled, I felt something begin to happen. A sensation unlike anything I had ever experienced began to overtake my body. In spite of all of the sensations that I had felt while doing ecstasy, I had never experienced anything like this. It was as if a weight was lifting from off of my body. The only way that I can explain it is that it was like a piece of cement eight inches thick and the length of my entire body was being lifted off me. It wasn't just an exterior sensation as though it were merely something external. I could feel a weight within me begin to lift as well. Have you ever been in a situation where once it is resolved you have a sense of relief overwhelm you? Well, that was what this was like, except this was no less than a hundred times more intense. It was so powerful that it would have been no different had there actually been something on top of me.

The uniqueness of the situation was not lost on me. I knew that what I was experiencing was a genuine sign from God. As I laid there in shock from what I was experiencing, the reason for the sign became clear. God had sent a clear sign to tell me that I had been forgiven. The sorrow in my heart immediately turned into joy. Instead of tears of sorrow, tears of happiness rolled from my eyes. For once in my life, I knew that everything was going to be OK. I didn't know how it was going to work out, but I knew that God would see me through it all.

The sensation was still there when I drifted off into a deep sleep. For the first time in my life, I knew what a hug from God felt like, and although it has been nearly ten years since that day, the sensation that I experienced is still fresh in my mind. It was yet another confirmation that God was calling me to Him.

To this date, I have never experienced anything similar to it. It is my belief that God knew that I needed some type of confirmation. Conversing with God about my sins had brought me into a deep state of sorrow, but the sensation of the weight of my sins being lifted from me allowed me to know that God not only existed, but that He rewarded those who genuinely sought Him.

When I awoke, the experience from the night before was still fresh in my mind. While all of the other men went to eat breakfast, when the doors were unlocked, I stayed in my cell, once again pouring my heart out to God.

However, this morning was different. Right before I had fallen asleep, my tears of sorrow had transitioned into tears of joy. For the first time in my entire life, I was confident that everything was going to be fine. I didn't know how, but I *knew* it anyway, and my faith wasn't a blind faith either. What I had experienced the night before combined with what God had shown me from my past had instilled within me a level of belief that I would not have had otherwise.

Though I didn't know how it was going to work out, I did know that God would see me through it all. And so, my life as a new person began.

I began my new life by starting my day in prayer. My morning prayer was not nearly as long as the one the night before had been. Once I finished, I started my day as I had all of the days that came before it. Even though the activities remained the same, I knew something had changed. Though it's true that I cannot identify how things were different, I will stake my life on the fact that I knew they were. I'm not saying that I woke up a "saint" as the world would define it, because I still found myself swearing, smoking, and carrying all of the other characteristics of a sinner, but unlike the day before, I now had a desire and power to live differently. I had no real understanding of what life would look like. I just knew what it would *not* look like.

Instead of trying to identify things that I should be, I decided to concentrate on the things that I knew God didn't want me to be. Strangely enough, though this whole situation was foreign to me, I knew that what I wanted was fully within my grasp. I knew that with Jesus in my life, I had what I needed to live the life that He intended me to live. The connection between heaven and myself, though long abandoned, had in a very short time begun filling me with hope, promise, and strength to fight the battles that awaited me.

Chapter 14

THAT ONE GIFT...

Every day we were allowed to wander the prison yard for about 35 minutes. As I walked around, I began wondering what the rest of my life would look like. Hate, anger, fear, and sorrow were everywhere. Sure, the men tried to mask it, but the more they attempted to cover it, the more desperate their situation appeared. For the sake of being honest, for the majority of my 25 years, I had been just as angry and hateful as they.

Psychology had always been a field of study that I appreciated. My reading had taught me that many emotions that we humans exhibit are merely other emotions that we had unknowingly repackaged. For instance, many people don't realize it, but anger is primarily fear turned outward. So, whenever I saw an angry person I simply asked myself, "What might he be afraid of?" For most of them, it was simply a fear of being seen as the vulnerable person that they were. We have such a "masculine" society that men are conditioned to act as though they are 10 feet tall and bulletproof. I too had been there, but my recent experiences brought home the reality that my life was only preserved by the grace of God.

Slowly, my understanding of who I had been versus who God had empowered me to be began to settle in. I went from thinking that my life was purposeless, to knowing that although I didn't have a clue what it would look like, God had something in store for me. God's love for me had revealed that He had a plan for me and that though it may not have been what I would have imagined for myself, that it was going to be better than anything that I could have ever imagined or effected for myself.

Day 18 in Quarantine arrived. I had finished all of the medical, psychological, and occupational testing that they wanted to do. As I sat in my cell, an officer approached the doorway and told me to pack up my belongings. I would be riding out in the morning. For security reasons, they didn't tell anyone where they were being transferred to, but we prisoners had our ways of knowing. It wasn't long and word came to me that I would be going to Riverside Correctional Facility (RCF).

RCF had an interesting history. In the past, it had been used to house youthful offenders, but now it was being used to house both conventional prisoners (serving sentences ranging from four years to life in prison) and the criminally insane. RCF operated a program called RTP (Resident Treatment Program). That is nothing but a fancy name for a Thorazine distribution unit. Thorazine is a pharmaceutical used to keep people pliable and tranquil. Most men seen for psychiatric issues are prescribed some sort of sedative or tranquilizer. It's obvious that this is the case because those who go to the medication line are sleeping 30 minutes after their return and don't wake back up until it's time to go get another pill. Many prisoners do their entire time in prison in this condition.

As expected, I was transferred to Riverside Correctional Facility. To be honest, I was surprised that they would send me there. I had grown up in this area and knew it like the back of my hand. On one occasion, I had used the prison parking lot as a place to snort a few lines of cocaine.

The streets that surrounded this prison were filled with the homes of lifelong friends and associates, so it didn't surprise me when, after getting through the intake process, one of the officers recognized who I was. I hadn't been in the unit for more than 20 seconds when the officer not only called me by name, but admitted that he knew my father's name as well.

As the initial weeks passed, I began getting used to my surroundings. Usually that would be a good thing, but my surroundings were filled with violence and guys who, while professing to understand respect, were nothing but disrespectful at the very core of their being. There were prisoners starting fires in the units, raping other prisoners, and stabbing one another on a regular basis. I was stuck in a cage surrounded by a brood of vipers.

All of the tactics that I had used to survive and elevate my position in the past, I could no longer implement. Manipulation had to take a back seat to submitting to God, but to be frank, I didn't really know how to submit my will to God. I had absolutely no clue what that looked like in the life of a believer. Sure, I grew up in a Christian home, but I was so far removed from a spiritual mindset that the concept of submission to God was like Greek to me. In many ways I was still doing things as I always had been, and I knew it. One of the things I did remember about my youth was something that I had learned about King Solomon, the richest man to have ever lived. I remembered that God had told him that He would give wisdom, knowledge, and understanding, and in the book of James, that promise has been given to everyone who would ask for these things. (1 Kings 4:29—34, James 1:5). So, in the mornings, I would ask God to give me knowledge, understanding, and wisdom. For some reason, even though I had no real "history" of walking with God, I trusted that the promise was true for me. Something deep inside me knew that God would fulfill that promise.

Time passed by, and before I knew it, nearly two months had transpired since I was transferred to Riverside. Thanks to the close proximity to my family, communication between my parents and me increased significantly. My brother and sister were still ignoring my attempts to reach out, but I had to respect their feelings. I had hurt them more than most. Their love and trust for me had been battered by what I had done. So, I decided to sit back and allow time to take its course. After a while, I was even able to receive a visit from my parents. In the conversations that I had with them, I told them about the decision that I had made, that I had embarked upon a journey with God into the unknown.

My parents remained reserved, knowing that I had made a lot of "decisions" in the past that never amounted to anything but a broken promise, but even with that said, they didn't want to let this opportunity pass by.

Time was beginning to move faster with each passing day. I began making acquaintances with some of the "lifers," and the conversations that I had with them really opened my eyes to what prison is like. There are multiple layers of reality in prison. There is what you think you see, there is what you actually see, and then there is what really exists. It is difficult to explain to someone who has not been there, but if you are reading this from inside a cell or a unit, you know exactly what I mean. Having that information meant absolutely nothing though unless I applied it to myself. I began soaking up all of the prison knowledge that I could, knowing that having this information would allow me to navigate within this environment without causing waves so to speak.

The fall of 2005 came in like a lion. One week it was 80 degrees and sunny while a week later it was 40 degrees at night, and the leaves were all changing color. About four months had passed since I had given my heart to God. Everything had been going as good as could be expected. I had had a few run-ins with other prisoners, but nothing serious. In the back of my mind I knew that something was about to happen. I had noticed a rhythm about life. When everything smoothes out, you better be watching for what's coming your way, because something is most certainly headed for you.

One day, while sitting on my bunk during count, I received a pass to go to the property room. Once count cleared, I got off of my bunk and walked over there. Shortly after approaching the counter, I was handed a brown paper bag. I signed for it, opened it, and pulled out a box. As I read the cover, a smile crossed my face, a smile from ear to ear.

My father had purchased a King James Version leather-bound Bible with H.M.S. Richards study aids. Though I tried not to let it show on the outside, I was so excited! I had wanted a Bible of my very own. All of the Bibles that I found in the prison were abused beyond belief, and the ones that weren't nearly destroyed were such simplified translations that the very depth of God's Word disappeared. On this day though, God had blessed me with a Bible that I knew I could use for years; a Bible that would turn out to be my support in times of distress, my sword when it came time to defend against error, and my source of strength in times of weakness.

It had been a really long time since I had smiled like that, but I knew that what I held in my hand was far more than a Bible. What I held in my hand was a sign that my parents were still standing behind me. That Bible indicated that someone believed that there was hope for me.

That gift my father gave me would be the very thing that nurtured my fragile walk with God. Like milk to a baby, the Bible helped me grow from an infant in God to a strong soldier in the Lord's army. That one gift changed not only my life, but the lives of many that I would encounter in the years to come.

Chapter 15

NO EXCEPTION

Time seemed to melt away at Riverside. December came, accompanied by long days of sitting on my bunk while the snow piled up outside. The arrival of the Bible couldn't have been better timed. I must admit, I was having a hard time grasping some of the stories and verses in it, but it wouldn't be long, and God would provide a solution to that difficulty. For now, I would have to move forward, prayerfully applying what I did understand.

As time passed by, I quickly discovered that a prisoner has to be watchful of dangers from every direction, even the staff. I had been at the compound for nearly six months when an officer approached me and told me that I had to pack up, that I would be leaving immediately.

The suddenness of it and the insistence in the officer's voice left me kind of speechless. For a few minutes, I almost wondered if the officer was messing with me. It wasn't completely unheard of. I had seen them convince the "fish" (the new guys) that there was a pool on the compound and that if they wanted to swim they had to sign the sign-up sheet. Of course, once they signed it, their names would be read off over the loudspeaker thus letting everyone know who the new gullible guppies were. This was different though, there was something else going on.

I listened to him and did as he had asked. I put all of my belongings into my duffle bag and then went to find out where he had gone. When I located him, I pulled him off to the side and asked him to tell me what was going on. In hushed tones, he told me that one of the officers on the compound was planning on setting me up, that he was going to try to make it look like I had broken into a secured area.

As he said it, I stood there shaking my head. It didn't even seem logical, but logic had nothing to do with it. The entire situation was motivated purely out of revenge. Apparently the officer had a lengthy history with my family, and this was his chance to get back at my loved ones without actually having to confront them. Classic passive-aggressive behavior.

There wasn't anything I could do. I didn't want to go to another facility, but the transfer had already been put in. The officer that I had been speaking to had approached the administration, discreetly warned them of what was going to happen, and filed the appropriate paperwork in order to get me on the next bus out of there.

THE STABBIN' CABIN

After leaving Riverside I made a short stop at Ionia Maximum Security Prison. The MDOC had planned on housing me there only to discover that a cousin of mine worked there as a guard. I left there on another van and headed to another prison located across the street. It was now obvious to the MDOC that they had to be selective about where they placed me. This last prison was the only one left in the area that I could actually be housed in. I had heard about this place, and none of it was good.

It was opened just a few years before, and when it was opened the prisoners christened it with the blood of those they didn't like. The bloodbath earned the facility the name of "The Stabbin' Cabin." It was more formally known as Bellamy Creek Correctional Facility. This prison featured both level two and level four prisoners. Three of the units were locked down for the majority of the day, while the other units were allowed access to the small yards located in the rear of the units.

I'll never forget walking into my unit for the first time. I had just finished walking with my property for what seemed like a half mile. As I entered the unit, I saw the officer stopping two guys who were coming in off of the small yard. He pulled them off to the side and did a random shakedown. It wasn't ten seconds later, and there on top of the counter were two eight-inch shanks. One had been retrieved from each of the prisoners. Both of the prisoners were handcuffed and sent off to the hole.

I slowly approached the desk and asked where I would be headed. The officer said, "Well, normally you would be going up to the first cell on the left, but you'll have to wait. We need to go up there and pack up some property. That was your bunky who was taken off in cuffs."

The officers eventually allowed me to go into the cell and pick everything up. Not an hour later, I had a new bunky moving in, and not two hours after that, I had another officer in my cell packing up the new guy's property. The new bunky had assaulted someone in the TV room downstairs. I just sat back and shook my head. I had seen a lot of stuff at Riverside, but I knew it wasn't going to measure up to what I would experience here.

In the first four days, I ended up going through five—count them, *five*—new bunkies. All of them ended up in the hole. Finally, on the evening of the fourth day, a third shift officer opened up my door and asked me who I was. He wanted to know why all of these guys were winding up in the hole. I explained that I had nothing to do with it. He then asked if I knew of anyone that I thought I would like to have move in. He said he was sick of printing off new name tags for the door. I smiled and gave him a name of a guy that I had met and thought that I would get along with, his name was Joey. The next morning, Joey was moving across the hallway into my cell. For once, I felt as though I could take a deep breath. The events of the last few days had instilled anxiety and a deep sense of uncertainty in me, and with this latest move, I felt like things would settle down.

Looking back at that whole situation, I believe that God was behind it all. Matter of fact, it is extremely difficult not to see the design in my life. Even though there was chaos all around me, I can see the Maker's handiwork all throughout those days—and the years to follow.

I settled into Bellamy Creek and tried to establish a routine. I wanted to craft my schedule in a way where I would have the least amount of interaction with others as possible. There were guys that I had known on the streets at this facility, but I knew that if I began hanging out with them I would find myself in the same situation that put me in here in the first place.

My parents had sent me some Christmas money, and with that, I purchased a TV. It was a 12-inch, black and white TV, but it was a TV nonetheless. It acted as a babysitter during the times when, for one reason or another, I couldn't read. However, I realized that the TV just didn't cut it for me. My mind was asking for a challenge. Nearly every day, I continued to pray for knowledge, wisdom, and understanding, and every day, I could feel the desire grow for something *more*, but as I looked around I didn't see anything that fit the bill, so to speak. Then one day during count, I heard the beautiful sound of the property officer calling my name over the loudspeaker. Every time I heard my name being called for property, I knew that my world was going to become a little bit better, that my journey was going to get a little more interesting. This time was no exception.

Chapter 16

A LESSON
FROM AGES PAST

The three-inch thick door to my cell rolled open as the officer activated its release. I walked down the stairs to the area where the officers were. It was there that they handed me another paper bag, but this one was heavy. I walked back upstairs with bag in hand. I wanted to wait until I got into my cell before I opened it. There were too many prying eyes in the unit. Guys were always waiting to find a reason to act stupidly.

Once the door closed behind me, I opened my package. I reached in and pulled out a handful of books, five in all. As I read the titles and the back covers, I recognized what they were. My father had sent me a copy of these same books the very first time I went to jail. I had never really paid them any attention the first time, but things were different this time.

As I shuffled the books in my hand, I realized that what my father had sent me would be the next step in my journey down my path with God. These books were a five-volume commentary on the Bible and Christianity. Written in the late 1800s these books were an incredible treasure trove of information.

I sat down and began reading them immediately. I opened the first volume titled *Patriarchs and Prophets* and started soaking in the material. Within ten minutes, I found myself drifting off into sleep. I felt this heavy weight on my eyelids coaxing me into this deep sleep. For me, this was strange because in order for me to sleep during the day, I had to be extremely high off of a "downer," or I had to have been deprived of sleep for several days. I chalked it up to being tired, closed the book, and decided to get some air.

Later that day I came back to the book and discovered that I experienced the same thing. For the next several days I found that every time I opened the books, sleep was soon to follow. At week's end, I called my father and thanked him for the books, but told him that I was having difficulty getting into them because of what was happening. His response was immediate. He said, "you're not tired, that's Satan trying to keep you away from what those books contain." I knew there was some truth to it because at that time, I was drinking about half a gallon of coffee a day, and prison coffee is akin to caffeinated mud. That liquid has such a kick that you could probably run a Formula-1 race car on the stuff.

My father's instructions were as follows, "Pray before you begin reading!" He told me that it was no different when I was studying the Bible. His words were, "Whenever you plan on entering into an experience with God, you should ask for His direction, guidance, and protection."

I had never thought about spiritual warfare affecting something as small as reading a book, but then again there were a lot of things that I had never considered.

After finishing our conversation, I hung up the phone and went back up-stairs to see if I could complete a chapter under the guidance of prayer. I prayed before I began, and strangely enough, I didn't feel weighed down by sleepiness. I actually finished the chapter with no problem. One thing I did notice was that my ability to read for any length of time, even apart from feeling sleepy, was difficult for me to do. I found my attention being diverted after only a few pages. I knew that in order for me to get through these books I would have to redevelop my study habits. As a child, I had excellent study habits, and now I would have to bring those back to the forefront in my life. Every day, I dedicated a portion of time to studying. I included Bible study, reading from the books my Father had purchased, and also reading from some other, non-religious sources of information. Many times, it would be an old National Geographic magazine.

It wasn't overnight, but in time my ability to stay engaged increased. I went from being able to read a couple of pages from each item to reading chapters from each source every day. I felt like the "old me" was beginning to return. My relationship with God got stronger as I really concentrated on what I was reading in my Bible. I realized that the verses I read contained an unexplainable characteristic. No matter how many times I had read a verse, when I reread the chapter, it was inevitable that I would find something new.

This verse said it all for me: "Open my eyes, that I may behold wondrous things out of your law [Word]" (Psalm 119:18 ESV). Whenever I opened the Bible with an intent to hear from God, He never let me down. I could hear His voice loud and clear. I didn't always want to hear what was said, but I knew that even if it wasn't what I wanted to hear, it was what I *needed* to hear.

I wasn't a perfect person; I'm still not perfect. Back then I had some very rough edges to my character. God would reveal things about myself that I needed to give up to Him, and in giving them up to Him, I discovered that my heart would change. How I saw life and how I looked at others around me began to change. It was slow and almost imperceptible, but when times of distress bore down on me, I could see the effect that my walk with God was having. I didn't respond as I had in the past. Even the "solutions" to the problem that came to mind were different. Usually, every time I was faced with a challenge, the solution—one way or another—involved someone getting hurt. However, now in distressful times, I felt patience or a calm settle over me. It wasn't as if it was incapacitating, only settling. It was just enough to help me stay even-keeled. I know that there were several times that had I not had this peaceful presence within, the choices that I would have made would have had disastrous results. Slowly and almost imperceptibly, I began to reflect Christ within me.

My walk with God saved my life several times throughout in the years. Bellamy Creek was a dangerous place for everyone there. I recall one day when an officer was responding to a fight at the end of the lower level. As he passed the second to last cells two men with weapons in hand came out from behind him. Each prisoner wielded a sock containing a padlock in it. The officer didn't stand a chance. The two guys who appeared to be fighting each other turned toward the officer and opened up on him. Within seconds the officer was fighting for his life.

It took support a long time to respond with a medical team. When they wheeled him out of there, most of us were certain that we would never see him again, and we were right. Incidents like this were common. Even going downstairs to use the kitchenette area was dangerous.

You never knew what someone else's agenda was. We all looked at each other as a threat because that is truly what we represented. Some of us were a physical threat, others were a financial or social threat. Life inside this prison was filled with hazards. At night, I would peer out from the small window next to my bed and watch as the flashing lights of the ambulance would come and go from Bellamy Creek and the other prisons that surrounded it. I would see the ambulance at our compound no less than three times a day. I even remember waking up to see a hearse from Lake Funeral Home parked next to my unit. Natural deaths occurred, but more often than not, men died from *other* causes.

Well, winter gave way to spring, and by the time the snow had melted, I had made it halfway through the first of the five books that my father had given me. Though the books were small enough to easily hold in your hand, the material was really deep, and by *deep* I mean that it made you stop and think. Most books that contain material like that are three-inch-thick reference books. The difference between those and what I was reading was that the books I held in my hand held my attention. At times I would be so deep in thought that I would lose all sense of my surroundings. Time would seem to disappear. I would look up from my book at the clock and find that it was almost time to walk to the chow hall. From the way the writer talked about God, I knew there was a lot more that I needed to learn. Stories about the men of old and what they were able to accomplish gave me strength. Joseph for instance was sentenced to serve seven years in an Egyptian prison after being wrongfully convicted for the crime of attempted rape, a crime that never occurred! But that prison sentence ultimately led to him being exalted so highly that he became the right-hand man of Egypt's Pharaoh.

If a little shepherd boy could be imprisoned and ultimately be given the keys to the most powerful kingdom in the world, then it's entirely possible that God could make the negative consequences of my past disappear as well. Clearly I would still have to serve my time, but it was then that I realized the powerful fact that my past did not have to dictate my future.

As the weeks passed by I continued reading through the Bible. In the morning, I would read from the series of books my father bought for me, and then periodically, I would climb up on my bunk and read random chapters in the Bible. Up until this point, I hadn't developed a way of systematically studying the Bible. It would be about another year before I felt comfortable enough with my Bible to study specific topics. In order to do that, I had to know where to find the topics, and that only came after I had memorized all of the names of the books of the Bible in their particular order. As a child I had memorized them, but over the years they had been lost along with many other important things.

A lesson from Ages Past

I had just begun to get settled into my routine, when, once again, I was told to pack up. By now you would think that I would have been used to hearing it, but when my name was called, only one thought circulated throughout my mind, and that was, "Where am I going now?"

The Stabbin' Cabin was the last prison in the Ionia area that I could be housed in. That meant that I would be transferred somewhere away from my family. My parents, who had recently decided to come see me on a regular basis, could no longer hop in the car, drive a few miles, and come see me when they wanted to. I immediately began asking God to be merciful on them. Personally, had it only been me, I could have cared less where they put me, but the last thing I wanted was for my parents to be further burdened by this experience—I had already put them through so much! Situations like these just made the whole experience that much more difficult for them to bear.

I gathered my property and waited for the officer to come to my cell in order to inventory it. Within a few minutes he was standing in my doorway with a transfer tag and paperwork in hand.

I couldn't help myself. I wanted to know two things. Firstly, why was I the only one being transferred? Secondly, where I was going?

As it turned out, I never did receive a conclusive reason as to why I was transferred, however, he did tell me where I was going. The officer told me that I would be going to Muskegon Correctional Facility (MCF).

Up until this time, I had been lying low. Over the last year, I had been acclimating myself to my surroundings. What I didn't know was that how I spent my time was about to change drastically. Bellamy Creek had been brutal; the violence that occurred there was animalistic. What I would see at MCF would take everything to a whole new level. I would be going from middle school straight to college. Class was now in session!

Chapter 17

KINDA LIKE COLLEGE...
BUT WITH BLOOD

I was getting pretty used to transferring from one joint to another. I had the whole process memorized, and I could tell that my comfort level in prison was getting increasingly higher. Now don't get me wrong, in no way am I saying that I was relaxed; I just wasn't jumping at every sound or moving blade of grass like some of the new guys coming in. I had seen enough in here to be able to identify a legitimate threat from someone who was just *trying* to intimidate with aggression.

Within a week, I was placed into a permanent cell, and I had an *OK* bunky. From the outside, everything looked fairly good. Actually, if you didn't know any better, you would have thought this facility was a college dorm. There were flowerbeds all around the units; a garden near the gym; a baseball and softball field in the yard. On top of that, there was a half-mile blacktopped running track out back.

Now, for all of you tax payers who are about to grab your torches and pitchforks—all of these things were paid for by the prisoners. Every prison operates a store so that prisoners can purchase deodorant, toothpaste, and food items. These stores are operated by the prisoners. Matter of fact, the prisoners actually employ several full-time citizens at each facility to supervise the operation.

The outward appearances were, of course, deceiving. The drug trade was incredible at this facility. Heroin, weed, meth, and ecstasy were all available to anyone who had the money, and of course, there were many men who, in spite of not having the money, still decided to use that which they couldn't afford. This led to beatings, stabbings, rapes, extortion, and murders. At night, I would have to make sure I put my glasses on when I went to the bathroom so that I wouldn't walk in the lines of blood formed by people bleeding as they went to or from the bathroom. I wish I were exaggerating, but I'm not. The saddest part is that after a while, I became desensitized to seeing both the events and the results of the events. Things would happen so often that when someone would get jumped in the bathroom, I wouldn't even stop brushing my teeth. I'd move if I had to, but for the most part, I knew that there was nothing that I could do to intervene so I just minded my own business.

Moments like that made me thank God for reaching out to me when He did. Had I not embarked on a journey with Him when I did, I probably would have found myself, in one way or another, involved in that garbage.

Two days after arriving at the facility I saw a sign stating that I could sign up for religious services, that there was a small Bible study group that met two times a week. Immediately, I signed up, and three days later, I was attending my first group Bible study since I had been a child. I was excited beyond words.

The day for the meeting arrived, and in walked four volunteers. I'll never forget their names: Gary, Jorine, Walt, and Jim. They walked in, introduced themselves, and started the Bible study. As they sang a song and started the service, I examined them closely. I could tell that these individuals actually loved what they were doing, but more importantly, I could tell that they actually cared for us. There was a genuineness about them that set me at ease.

While at this facility, my time studying the Bible increased significantly. What I noticed was that, as the environment around me became increasingly worse, my time spent in God's Word would grow. In the span of a year and a half, I had become somewhat biblically proficient. My studies, combined with reading the commentary set that my father had given me, had educated me to such a degree that I could now sit down and have a doctrinal discussion with nearly anyone. I was shocked at how much I had learned in such a short time. As I sat back and assessed the situation, I realized that this was the fulfillment of God's promise, the promise that He would provide knowledge, understanding, and wisdom to anyone who would ask for it.

Just 18 months before, I had been shooting Fentanyl and cocaine into my veins on a daily basis, and here I was now, having deep theological and philosophical conversations with officers and prisoners alike. The miracle was not lost on me or those who were familiar with where I had come from. My co-defendant—the one who had prevented me from getting to the gun on the morning of my arrest—arrived on the compound after being convicted for cashing bad checks. Despite our similarities in the past, it was as if we barely knew each other now. I wasn't better than him in any way, I was just, well, different.

Two years after having been arrested, I decided to be baptized. By this time, I had quit smoking and swearing. I had prayed for Christ to give me the power to overcome those habits, and I walked forward in faith, believing that I had received that strength. To this day, I have not touched a cigarette, and it has been eight years.

On a cool fall morning, I took the dip in a baptismal tank located under a stand of birch trees near the prison's yard. I knelt down in the water and tearfully confessed my faith in what Christ had done for me some 2000 years ago, dedicating my life in service to Him. I died, was buried, and resurrected in the waters of baptism that day. I didn't feel any sensations or experience anything supernatural, but when I walked back to my unit, I knew that if I continued to give God the glory and relied on His power, His Strength, and His will, that my life would be eternally altered. A voice inside me assured me that God had a plan for me. From that day on, I began actively seeking God's will for my life.

My baptism had been a pivotal part in my new life, but it didn't mean that my environment changed. I witnessed a lot of things first hand at that facility. On multiple occasions men tried to murder several of my friends, and several times, they nearly succeeded. I wasn't immune from the violence either.

One afternoon, I was surprised by a grown man standing at my doorway crying. There he was, holding a bunch of food and a dozen other things. I opened the door, and as tears rolled down his face he handed me the items and walked away. I yelled after him to see what was going on, but was left standing there in my cell. Shortly after that, one of the leaders of the Moors (a type of Islamic religious group) approached me and pulled me to the side. He began the conversation by telling me that he appreciated having me around the unit, that I brought smiles and humor to a place that rarely experienced comedic relief. I had never seen myself as "that guy," but I was happy to see that my personality had brought some sense of normalcy to an environment that rarely experienced happiness.

He continued by telling me that a prisoner who bunked with one of my friends had planned on jumping me in the weight pit that afternoon. He said that when it was brought to his attention, he immediately took care of it. I was then instructed that when the prisoner approached me, I was to accept whatever items he offered. I told him that the prisoner had already stopped by. The Moor's leader turned away, smiling approvingly.

After our conversation I asked another Moor that I knew what had happened. He said that they had sent well over a dozen men into the bathroom to "talk" with the guy who had planned on assaulting me. He was told that he would never lay a hand on me and that he was to take everything that he owned and hand it over to me within ten minutes or face the consequences. Apparently he got the point because he didn't hesitate to follow through.

Within two days, my would-be assailant approached me and formally apologized. I accepted his apology and told him that I would return his property, but I told him that if he wanted to remain breathing that he would have to make sure that nobody ever found out about it.

That situation showed me something interesting. I saw that God was using a Muslim individual—whom most Christians would never consider to be a friend or ally—for my protection. The whole thing was a lot to process. It raised a hundred and one questions, but I finally saw that if I over thought it, the situation would lose the impact that it was meant to have on me.

. . . .

After having been at Muskegon Correctional for a year, I was transferred yet again to another facility. This time it was due to my security level being lowered. I had managed to stay out of trouble, and so they decided to reward me by sending me to a prison that housed the men in dormitory-style units. The units consisted of 20 cubes that each held eight men. We were crammed into confined spaces, and that made for some very dangerous conditions.

However, when I was transferred this time, something inside me changed. I came to the realization that after each of these transfers, something significant would happen in my life to where I would subsequently be drawn into a closer relationship with God. Once I understood that, I began looking at the situation no longer in the negative, but as an opportunity. It was then that I realized that every challenge we encounter in life is designed to teach us a spiritual lesson. Unfortunately, the majority of time, we tend to overlook the lesson that God intends for us to learn. God then has no alternative but to allow us to experience yet another situation in which we have the opportunity to learn the spiritual (or character enriching) lesson that He feels we need to learn.

At the end of the day, our entire life is nothing but an opportunity for us to reestablish the relationship with God that was destroyed through sin. Many people think that the road ends when we ask Christ to come into our hearts, but that couldn't be further from the truth. The fact is that Christ coming into our hearts is but the beginning. Once He enters our hearts, the real work begins.

Chapter 18

BACK TO JACKSON

The next facility that I was sent to was named Cooper Street Correctional. Located in Jackson, Michigan, this facility was a level one minimum-security institution. In many ways, this facility was different from any that I had ever been to. The attitude of the staff was far more aggressive and disrespectful of the men that were housed there. This disrespect created an atmosphere of contention within the units, but I must admit that some of the prisoners didn't do much to neutralize it.

Once I got situated in my unit, I sent a letter to the chaplain in order to see if I could get signed up for a religious service. When he called me out, I discovered that there were no other prisoners signed up to attend the same group. The chaplain told me that although policy required him to have five men enrolled in order to have a meeting, he would allow me to have access to a private room twice a week for personal worship and study. I was excited because this would give me a place to do my Bible study without being interrupted by arguments, loud sports enthusiasts, or people who just wanted to make noise (and there are always a lot of those).

When I went to the room designated for the religious service group, I discovered that there was a cabinet containing some study material. I went through the books and saw that there was a small Bible dictionary, a concordance, and then I saw something odd.

On the bottom shelf, sat two large rectangular boxes each 2 feet long, 10 inches wide, and 6 inches thick. I pulled them out and saw that they contained two different sets of VHS tapes. I went to the officers' station and requested the use of a TV and VCR. Usually there was at least one available in the programs building for use in the classrooms where they taught the GED classes. The officer nodded, walked down the hallway and came back with a cart containing the items.

I went to the room and put the first tape into the VCR. As it started, a graphic came across the screen explaining which ministry was presenting the material. The ministry was named Amazing Facts, and the speaker was Doug Batchelor. I had never heard of either of them, but the series looked like it was going to cover a lot of material, so I sat back and prepared to take notes as the program commenced.

As Pastor Bachelor presented the topic, I became amazed. I had never seen someone on TV present the Scriptures so simply. He allowed the Bible to speak for itself, and in cases where there were difficult verses, he would go to other areas of the Bible; and those verses would give clarification on the challenging sections being studied. This was the first time I realized that the Bible should be used to define itself. A lot of pastors would utilize culture or outside sources to define portions of Scripture that presented a little difficulty, but the correct way was to allow the Word of God to define itself.

Week after week, I watched those videos. Eight times a month, I would go there and soak up all of the "Biblical goodness" that I could get. Since there were only two sets of VHS tapes, the day came when I had to replay the series again, but it didn't matter. The material was deep enough to where I would pick up on things the second time that I never saw the first time.

One day, after watching the video, I decided to write the ministry. At the end of the video, the contact information would display. This time, I paused it in order to write down the address. That night, I wrote them a letter and placed it in the mail. Their video offered study guides, so I wrote to them, asking if I could join their correspondence Bible study course. Within three weeks of mailing my letter, I received my first study. I sat down, read the questions, studied the passages, and filled out the answers before mailing the answer sheet back in.

Every other week I would receive a new Bible study, and interestingly enough, I could see my understanding of the Scriptures growing by leaps and bounds. I used the study guides as a start, but continued to research each topic all throughout the Bible on my own.

Because of Amazing Fact's faithfulness to the Scriptures, and their willingness to send me the Bible studies, a deep respect for them was established. They could have been like many other TV ministries and taught what they thought people wanted to hear, but they didn't.

I had seen other ministers on TV, had read their material, and found them to be poorly grounded in the Word. Many times, they did what I call "cherry picking." They would pull a verse from the surrounding context and manipulate it to mean what they wanted; but Amazing Facts made sure to include all of the material around it, and in addition to that, they studied the areas of the Bible that covered the same span of time or topic. Within a year of being at Cooper Street, I had gone from being an amateur to being proficient on many biblical topics. I not only saw my understanding of the Bible grow, I also realized that God was giving me opportunities to share what I was learning with both prisoners and officers.

One such day, as I sat in a quiet area of the unit, an officer from an adjoining unit noticed that I was studying my Bible. I had just gotten to Cooper Street, so I was not familiar with this officer. He continued going past me, walking through the passage that connected the two units, but he was so curious as to what I was doing that he came back to my unit and sat down at my table.

He asked me why I wasn't making some extra money like the other prisoners. I told him that today was the Sabbath, and since it was the day of rest, I didn't work. See, on Saturdays, all of the other laundry men (which is what I was) would use that day as a time to make some additional money by doing personal loads of laundry for the men at a price. On an average Saturday, they could pull in close to 15 dollars which was a lot of money in prison.

He then began asking questions about the Sabbath. He had always believed that the seventh-day Sabbath was on Sunday. That morning, we began talking about the topic and didn't stop. He had never understood the subject as I had presented it, so he asked question after question. As he asked questions, I noticed that the locations of the verses that I needed to answer his questions would immediately come to mind. This would have been an example of recall had it not been for the fact that I had never come across these verses in the short time that I had been studying. The verses that I read to him were verses that directly answered his questions.

I felt as though something was working with me to guide this officer into a deeper understanding of God's Word. He was so engaged in the discussion that after leaving to do his rounds, he would come right back to continue the discussion. For nearly his entire eight-hour shift, we spoke about the Bible and what it taught about the Sabbath.

When it was all said and done, I realized what had occurred. The Holy Spirit had used me to reach this officer. It was after that, that I was told by a fellow officer that the individual that I had been talking to was the pastor of a local church. He was bi-vocational which meant that he worked a normal job during the week but pastored a church when he wasn't working a nine-to-five position at the prison.

I was taken aback by that fact because this guy had clearly been studying his Bible for *far* longer than I had been, but in spite of that, *I* was the one showing him what it taught. I quickly saw that God was using me as a vessel, but I also understood that God would only continue to use me in this way if I acknowledged that what was occurring was only happening because it was Him at work *in* me.

God gave me multiple opportunities to minister at Cooper Street, and with that ministry came opposition by Satan. Satan could see what was happening in the hearts of those that I worked with, and he hates losing hard-earned souls, especially with the help of someone whom he once had full control over—me.

It wasn't uncommon for people to be disrespectful to me because of my faith, but I simply saw it as proof that I was on the right track. In spite of the occasional problem, God continued to elevate me on the compound. For instance, every unit is allowed to have two prisoners represent them before the warden's administration. Once a month, we would meet with the warden and facility department directors in order to discuss ways that we could better work with each other.

One evening, I had just returned from a warden's meeting when I noticed that the entire unit was in an uproar. As soon as I walked into the lobby I could tell that something was *seriously* wrong. The tension was so thick and the pressure so great that it was difficult to breathe.

I walked up to someone and asked him what was happening. He told me to go find Tony, and he would fill me in on the details. Now, Tony was a laid-back guy who never bothered anyone. He was light-hearted and wanted nothing more than to do his time in peace. Guys like him were a great asset in an environment full of predators.

I found Tony and asked him what had happened. He told me that a few weeks prior, his aunt had submitted a visitor's application so that she and Tony's daughter would be able to come see him. He had not heard anything concerning whether it had been processed and approved, so he decided to go ask our Assistant Resident Unit Supervisor (ARUS) about it. Now, the ARUS was the one person who held the majority of power in the unit. He or she determined where you worked, slept, and essentially, where you did your time. They could send you to a prison camp in the frigid Upper Peninsula if they wanted to, so typically they acted as if they were God on earth. This particular ARUS was no different.

When Tony had walked in there, he noticed another prisoner sitting in the ARUS's office with a pile of forms on his lap. These forms were obviously the visitor applications, phone lists, catalog order forms, parole paperwork, and other legal documents that the ARUS was responsible for processing. This was obvious by the varying colors of the paperwork. These forms all came in triplicate and were all multicolored.

Tony looked at the prisoner and then turned his attention to the ARUS, inquiring as to the status of the application. Upon mentioning his aunt and daughter, the prisoner sitting to his left said, "Your daughter's name is beautiful."

Now, up to this point, Tony had never mentioned his daughter's name. He swiftly turned his attention to the prisoner and asked him how he knew. In response, the prisoner pulled Tony's aunt's visitor application from the pile. This incensed Tony.

On that application was all of his aunt's personal information: her name, address, phone number, birth date, driver's license number, and a slew of other details. What was supposed to be strictly confidential information, was now in the hands of another prisoner. This put both his daughter and aunt in great danger—and Tony knew it. Not wanting to jeopardize his chance of seeing his daughter, Tony left the office without incident, but upon returning to his bunk, he began burning with anger.

Everyone around him couldn't help but notice that the well-mannered Tony was not his usual self. Once the other prisoners found out what had happened, they began getting angry, and with every passing minute the tension in the building increased. By the time I had heard all of the details, the unit officers had actually locked themselves in the office.

The ARUS was completely oblivious to what was taking place. I found the other unit representative, and together we went into the ARUS's office. I told her that what she had done had unnecessarily caused a dangerous situation—both for the citizens who had submitted those forms and for the prisoners in the unit. I told her that the person she had given the forms to had not been given the clearance necessary to see such information. Matter of fact, there was no position on this compound that would have given that type of information to a prisoner.

She looked at me with disdain and told me to get out of her office. I said, "You have an opportunity to diffuse this situation. If you don't do something, it will leave me no choice but to find an alternative method of taking care of the problem."

She replied by saying, "Do what you feel you need to do—now get out of my office."

I walked out of there and approached the officer's station. They opened the door, and I told them what had happened. I also told them that because of her actions, I would need to speak to the shift commander on duty. The officers didn't hesitate to give me the information. They even called the sergeant and told him that I was on my way. I followed policy and went through the chain of command so as to leave no loophole by which the ARUS could get out from under the action that I was about to take.

Upon hearing the details of the situation, the shift commander told me to go ahead and file a grievance against the ARUS. I walked back to the unit and found my bunky who just so happened to be a legal secretary. He knew Michigan Compiled Law very well, and I happened to know MDOC policy and procedure like the back of his hand. I had spent quite a bit of time studying the policies of the Michigan Department of Corrections because I knew that if I understood the policies that governed the prisons, I would have a better chance of not being abused by the staff that believed they could act with impunity.

That night, I prayed and asked God for guidance. Had this been a matter of putting only myself at risk, I would have walked away from the situation; but I wasn't the only one in harm's way. I had been appointed to represent my unit, and with that came certain responsibilities. Too many men had allowed things like this to go by unchecked because they knew that retaliation would soon follow their actions. I was more worried that the unchecked actions of the ARUS would lead to increasingly dangerous behavior. So, in the morning—after my personal devotions and prayer time—I went to the law library and spoke to the clerk. I knew he was proficient in the MDOC Employee Handbook, so I asked him to help me draft a grievance against the ARUS. When we were finished with our project, we were in possession of a powerful piece of work that I knew would draw a lot of attention.

We submitted the grievance that afternoon, and within a day, it was already having an effect. The warden came into our unit, wondering why an inspector from the MDOC headquarters in Lansing (the state capital) was calling for a response. Because of what I asserted in the grievance, the form was sent directly to the top. In the grievance, I charged the ARUS with dereliction of duty, conduct unbecoming of a state employee, endangering the safety of the public, and endangering the security of the facility. I cited Michigan Compiled Law, and then quoted from the MDOC Employee Handbook that stated that the MDOC was bound to enforce the law.

You can imagine the impact that something like this would have on everyone involved. The warden was upset that dirt from within his facility was exposed externally; the officers were scared that they might have been included in the grievance; and the ARUS, well, as you can imagine, the ARUS was not happy with me. I knew that they would eventually retaliate, and in time they did.

The ARUS was removed from my unit and suspended for a short time, but the joke was ultimately on me. Once 90 days had gone by, I was on a transport to a prison located in the Upper Peninsula. They waited 90 days so that I couldn't accuse them of direct retaliation. I knew it was coming though. I was aware that my actions would have consequences, but what I didn't realize is how God would use that to His benefit.

While in the Upper Peninsula, I was transferred to two facilities within a week before finally getting a chance to unpack my property. I was convinced that this was part of the plan to retaliate against me, but in retrospect, I believe it was just the result of the disorganization within the MDOC. I finally settled at a small minimum-security compound nestled in some pines outside of Iron River, Michigan.

While there, I did as I had been doing for the last two years. I started doing Bible study with men who were interested in drawing closer to God. Men who wanted a better life joined our study, and at times, officers would sit within earshot in order to listen in on what was being said.

The distance away from my family made me long to see them. This brought out other questions about my future. For the first time since my arrest, I began wondering what my life would be like once I got out. I wondered whether or not God would bring someone into my life as a wife, and if so, who would it be?

Usually, these types of questions would go just as quickly as they had come, but this one would not leave. Would I ever get married? Is there anyone that I know that God would bring into my life as a partner? As I contemplated these questions, I couldn't help but indulge in thoughts about my past. I had met a lot of women, but there were hardly any that I felt had the qualities that a man would hope to see in a wife—all of this stemming from the perspective of who I used to be. Now that Christ came into the picture, the requirements that a woman would have to meet became much different than what I used for picking out a girlfriend in the past.

Once I examined my past relationships, I only found one person that might be a potential candidate, and it was someone that—in spite of all the insanity of my past—I actually loved. That person was Brenda. The girl whom I'd met at Arby's. The girl who originally hated my guts was the one person that I could actually envision marrying. With that in mind, I walked down the hallway and called my mother.

Just three years before this day, I had betrayed the trust and love of my mother by breaking into her home. By this time, God had not only brought us back together, but had also helped us build a relationship that was stronger than ever. When she picked up the phone, I asked her to do whatever she could to track down Brenda's address. I didn't tell her what God had put on my heart; I simply asked her to see if she could track her down. She said she would see what she could do.

The next morning I called her again, and to my surprise, my mother had found three addresses. I went back to my cell, pulled out a notebook, and wrote three identical letters. I received a response eight days after having mailed the letter. Amazingly, one of the letters had found Brenda, and after three long years of separation, we were reconnected.

In that letter Brenda told me how good it was to hear from me. She told me that the word on the street was that years ago I had been killed at Bellamy Creek. She told me what had been going on in her life and what her goals were now. Interestingly enough, what I noticed in her letter was that she, too, had been on a journey of self-improvement. Though I had no idea what would ultimately happen, I could see possibilities for the two of us; but I also knew that I couldn't get my hopes up too high.

Starting, developing, and maintaining a relationship where one of the individuals is incarcerated is extremely challenging. In order for it to be successful, each person has many sacrifices that have to be made. They have to sacrifice what their ideal relationship would be. They have to sacrifice privacy because all of your letters and phone calls are screened, and in addition to that, the person on the outside has to sacrifice the physical companionship that comes from having someone there to hold, comfort, and support you during the tough times in life.

At first, Brenda and I could only write each other. It wasn't until six months after our first correspondence, that we were finally able to begin calling each other on the phone. Then, almost a year after we were first reconnected, we were able to see each other in person. Once again, the MDOC transferred me. This time it was to a facility outside of Grayling, Michigan. Though it was a three-hour trip to the facility from where Brenda lived, it was still close enough for her to drive.

I must admit that the first visit was a little awkward. It had been a long time since we had seen one another, and we were both completely different people at that point. We had our memories to rely on, but those memories were of times past that weren't something to be proud of. We had to create new memories and develop new ways to communicate that were constructive and healthy.

As our time together increased and familiarity grew, our comfort level with one another increased more and more. Those months in Grayling worked as a good buffer for us. The facility was far enough away where we couldn't see each other too often, but it was close enough to where we could comfort one another in person.

Being in a relationship with me was difficult for Brenda. She faced criticism from her mother, her sister, her brother-in-law, and many of those who claimed to be her friends. In general, society stigmatizes anyone who has a criminal record, and while I can see why they do that, the stigmatization should not transcend onto the person who chooses to love that individual. Brenda was facing a lot of criticism, yet she stood firm. She openly acknowledged her love for me to anyone who asked. I could see that dedication, and I determined to do my very best to support her and reward her for what she had done for both our relationship and me.

Chapter 19

HIT SQUADS AND FOLDED HANDS

I t wasn't long before, once again, I was transferred. This time, it was because the facility (and several others like it) was being closed. God had His hand in the move as He had in all of the others. Instead of being transferred to facilities far away from home (as nearly all of the other prisoners were), I was transferred back to a facility in Muskegon, just 75 minutes from where Brenda lived.

Our visits increased to nearly two a week, and our phone calls were occurring daily. We would study the Bible on her visits, and I could see that God was working mightily in her life as He was in mine. We were growing together, facing challenges and obstacles with Christ, and enjoying the victories that came as a result to trusting in Him. When I was with her, it was easy to forget that I was still incarcerated.

In spite of being in prison, I was completely happy. The day came when I obtained a clearer view of my life. There was once a time when I thought my life was hopeless, that there was no point in living any longer. I had once believed that what I had done was so bad that nobody would ever accept me, but here I was just a few years later, a completely different man. I had become a man of hope, contentment, and optimism.

The relationships that had been destroyed were reestablished. God had brought them back together in such a way that they were stronger than they had ever been. In addition to that, God had given me a faithful wife to treasure, protect, and support. I had what I had always been searching for in power, drugs, and money; I had happiness, purpose, and hope for the future.

By this time over four years of my sentence had gone by, which meant that I could be released in about 3 years. It was incredible to see the change that had occurred in such a relatively short amount of time, and though I could see it, it was still difficult to fathom. How could growth so drastic take place in someone who, at one time, had been so broken? You hear about people claiming to have changed, only to see later that it was all a show. I had seen many of those situations occurring on a weekly basis. During a visit, it was common to see guys holding a Bible while talking with their wife, mother, or girlfriend; but while in the unit, they would be no different than they were when they first came to prison. Sometimes they had become far worse than they had been when they were first incarcerated. Some of the most wicked men in prison were those who tried to act like saints in the visiting room. But as it is with most charades, anyone with any genuine life experience could see through the lie. When it came to me, though, I knew that I was different and so did those who were close to me now. Even those who had been close to me in the past knew that I was not the same person. Officers and MDOC staff regularly asked me why I was even in prison. When staff at the prison are telling you that you don't belong there, you know something miraculous has happened, and something miraculous had happened. God had changed this leopard's spots.

As my life began to change, I began wondering what I needed to do in order to prepare for my future. I did not want to be paroled from prison without having a job; so, I contacted James, the owner of the restaurant that I had managed prior to going on the run, and he told me that if a position was open upon my release, that he would give me a job. With that arranged, I felt as though I had everything set up.

By this time Brenda and I had been together for nearly a year. There was no mistaking where I thought God was leading us, and after much prayer I told Brenda that it was my intention to marry her. I had brought the subject up in the past, but this was when there was a sense of determination expressed. Brenda and I discussed it, and after praying about it, we decided to get married once I was released.

We both loved each other and knew that, after what we had been through, the natural thing to do was to dedicate our lives to serving God as one. We knew that God meant for us to be husband and wife. We could see His orchestration in our lives, and I felt honored to be chosen by God to be her husband. For us, it was the natural choice.

As time passed by, the transfers to prisons across Michigan continued. At each prison I would begin organizing and operating Bible studies. I watched as men began to get familiarized, not only with the Bible, but with Christ. My heart reached out to these men. I knew what Christ could do for them. Some of these men had pasts that were far worse than mine. I met one man that had been abused by both his mother and sister for his entire childhood. He had carried those memories, thoughts, and experiences throughout his life and marriage, until eventually, it manifested itself in the lives of his own children when he abused them as he had been abused.

It would have been easy for me to look at this man with the same contempt and hate as nearly every other individual did, but instead of seeing him for what he had done, I saw him for what he could be in Christ. My concern for him didn't justify his crimes or minimize his sins. I was just as disgusted as anyone else for what he had done, but one thing my past taught me was that at the end of the day, we aren't all that different. In some ways we are all the same. The Bible states it like this, "the wages of sin is death," "for all have sinned and fall short of the glory of God," we will all experience the same end: eternal death.[1]

Although our sins may be different, the results are all the same. What we did, in the grand scheme of things, is irrelevant in that we will all die an eternal death unless we take advantage of the way out that God has provided. Understanding sin in this way allowed me to reach out to those who had committed the most terrible sins. Those who have committed the worst sins are also those who are under the most guilt and in need of the most forgiveness.

Months continued to go by, and as the end of my prison sentence drew closer, I knew that the devil would make my life increasingly difficult. Once again I was transferred and when I arrived at the latest correctional facility, someone that I had known at an earlier prison said that he was going to get me a job at a MSI (Michigan State Industries) textile factory. MSI is an organization operated by the State of Michigan, and it utilizes prisoners for their work force. MSI had several different factories, each producing various types of products. Some may make clothing, some shoes, while others produce cos-

---

1 Romans 6:23; 3:23 NKJV

metics or metal products like road signs or license plates. The factory at this facility was responsible for making t-shirts, socks, and underwear. Within the week, I received a pass to go to work at the factory. I had never operated a sewing machine, but I knew that if I was going to work there that I would have to learn and learn quickly.

The morning of my first day came. I joined about 40 other men, and after an initial search, we all boarded a bus to the site where the factory was located. The ride took about five minutes since the factory was only about half a mile from the main housing units. Upon arrival, we were all ushered into the bottom of the building where we all had to strip and walk through a metal detector.

Once through the metal detector, we walked through the doorway of an adjoining room where we were allowed to dress in two-piece uniforms and put on a pair of flip-flops. From there, we had to walk in the dark basement for the entire length of the building. Occasionally, you would feel a cockroach the size of a small mouse scurry over your foot. Once in a while, you would hear them go skidding across the floor as people accidentally kicked them while walking in the dark. What can I say, but "Welcome to prison!"

God had been blessing me all throughout my prison experience, and this was no different. The department I was placed in was the one that produced men's underwear. The underwear were for prisoner use within the MDOC, and the remaining supply was sold to non-profits and/or prisons across the country. What made this situation a blessing from God was the individual supervising my department.

First impressions are usually correct, and when I met her I was definitely impressed. She had a powerful presence and the way she carried herself was worthy of respect. I could tell that she had been working in this environment for a long time because she knew how to communicate in a way that made us want to work with her and not merely for her.

What impressed me the most is that during the day, she didn't just walk around barking orders, but from the minute we started to the minute we stopped, she was working right next to us. Not only was she working, but she was working just as hard as we were, and that made us want to work that much harder. Rarely had I ever seen anyone like her in the MDOC. The only people that I had ever seen carry themselves like this were Christians. It was an interesting observation. The Christian individuals who worked in the department of corrections had great work ethic. They carried themselves in a way that made others want to work in a supportive capacity.

After working in this factory for a week, you could see that nearly every prisoner in her department would not only stand up for her, but put their lives on the line for her. We were very protective of her, and it wasn't because she practiced favoritism or broke the rules, it was because you could tell that she would never ask you to do something that she was not willing to do herself, and if something happened and you were being wrongfully accused by an officer, she would defend the prisoner at the expense of being spurned by her fellow staff.

One day, I gathered up the courage to go sit across from her and ask her whether or not she was a Christian. I sat down and began assisting her by collecting and organizing the pieces that she had finished sewing. I finally broke the ice by telling her that after working there for a period of time, I could tell she was different. When asked as to whether or not she was a Christian, she confirmed that she was and that she and her husband were Methodists. She continued explaining that, like me, her husband was a serious student of the Bible. I knew right then that if he and I ever met, we would be good friends.

Over the months that we worked together in that factory, we developed a mutual trust. She knew that she could count on me to do my job to the best of my ability, and I trusted that she would do hers in the same manner. Our department regularly produced higher than expected numbers, and I knew that it was attributed to her leadership. Unfortunately, the same could not be said for the other departments in our factory.

In the end, our factory was closed down, and many of the prisoners who worked there lost their jobs. I, however, was transferred to another factory in yet another prison. My supervisor had transferred to another assignment at a prison across the road, and she decided to transfer me as well. I knew her decision to transfer me was based on two primary factors. The first was that I not only knew how to operate a sewing machine, but I was a good worker. The second was that she knew that she could trust me. She was about to go into an environment where nobody knew her. By having me there, I could speak up for her in situations where she was not able to speak for herself. And so, I was transferred to another prison. I hoped that this one would be my last.

When I transferred to this latest facility I was within nine months of my seven-year minimum. However, I still had to see the parole board. Nothing was ever written in stone, and I still faced an entity that had no knowledge of the changes that had happened in my life while in prison. During the six and one half years that I had been in prison, I had never received a ticket for misconduct. However, in the parole boards' eyes, that is not necessarily a positive thing.

I have known individuals who were not granted parole because the parole board felt that they had found a way to manipulate both the system and those whom they had come in contact with. Many people think it's impossible to truly change; and the members of the parole board are no different. For many people, Christianity is just a tool that prisoners use to manipulate others. With this in mind, my anxiety began to grow significantly worse as the interview date with the parole board drew closer.

Life at the new facility was like living at nearly every other prison. There were assaults, attempted murders, and every other thing that comes with living in a prison. As soon as I arrived on the compound I was assigned to work in the factory, and after working in the new department for a couple of weeks—everything seemed to be going well.

Life wasn't complete without Bible study, so I managed to start a new study on the book of Daniel with some of the guys who were meeting regularly for worship in the programs building. When I first joined the group and organized the study, we had nine men who were signed up, and by the time we finally began, the number had nearly doubled. I could see God working in a mighty way on this compound.

Rarely had I ever seen so many men that were selflessly seeking Truth, but with sincere seekers comes opposition. I knew the devil would try to ruin it somehow. In the past he had utilized the administration or chaplain to shut things down, and I expected no less this time around. However, I never imagined that the upcoming obstacles would be as extreme as what there were.

In the weeks that I had been working in the new factory, several things became clear. For one, I was the only white guy working in the department; and while in the free world that makes very little to no difference, in prison, that can mean everything. I could handle guys making me feel uncomfortable, I was used to feeling "out of place." Usually, though, once guys got to know me, that type of behavior would disappear.

The second obstacle I was facing was that there were no other Christian prisoners working in the department. In fact, the religious majorities were either Moors or part of the Nation of Islam. Now, while many of the men in these organizations may be respectful of your individual practices, some are not. Fortunately, nearly all of the individuals in this department were not only respectful, they were also educated, intelligent, and articulate.

The threat would come from someone within the group that I did not expect. One of the men who had recently started in the department was having difficulties operating the sewing machines. He would break needles or reconfigure the settings of the components on a daily basis.

These situations would put the entire operation behind, and it would drastically reduce the productivity. My supervisor was weighing the option of replacing him, and although she hadn't said it directly, I knew his day was coming.

One day after lunch, I leaned into the doorway of her office and told her that I would start training him so that steady progress, as a whole, could be made again. That afternoon I sat down with him and attempted to show him how to operate the machine. The results were terrible. In that one sitting, he had managed to break two needles. This was a costly mistake seeing as how the needles for these machines had to be shipped in from a special supplier. This guy got so upset that he just gave up. I knew not to push him, as it would only escalate the situation. I decided to let the dust settle, and the next day, when we had a chance, I would try to go back at it.

The next morning, one of the most respected men on the compound—a member of the Nation of Islam—came and told me that the guy that I had been helping, Anthony, had put a hit out on me. He said that he did what he could do to stall it, but in about 24 hours the hit would go active. He added, "Whatever you are going to do, you had better do it quick."

It wasn't uncommon for guys to pay others to have someone gutted. On the compound, we called it a "honey bun hit," because it only took about $50 worth of store goods to get someone killed. There were so many men who had nothing, that the possibility of getting a $50 store bag was enticing. Normally, men in this situation would do one of two things. Either they would get a few shanks, a couple of friends, and go take the threat out themselves, or they would go tell a staff member about the threat and then lock up for security. Neither of those were an option for me. I had gone nearly seven years without having to gut anyone, and after what I had seen in prison, I certainly didn't feel comfortable notifying the administration. Doing that was no different than telling another enemy that you were vulnerable.

Some may say that I should encourage people to go tell the authorities when they face a threat, but in prison, many times the authorities pose a threat as well. Of course, they aren't always a direct threat, but their practices do not protect those prisoners who risk their lives (and the lives of their families) by giving up information in exchange for safety. I had seen individual after individual go that route only to be faced with a much worse situation in the end.

Once I found out about the hit, I asked my supervisor for the day off. I went back to the unit and immediately called home. Though I knew I couldn't tell them anything about the hit, I knew that I needed them to be praying, so I asked my parents and Brenda to pray for me. It killed me that I couldn't go into detail, but I knew if I did, they would in-turn contact the administration, and then I would be in all sorts of garbage. It would only make the situation ten times worse.

I hung up the phone, went back to my cell, and did exactly as I had asked my family to do. For hours I asked God for direction, for protection, and for peace through the storm. Though I had been in dangerous situations in prison, this was the only one where I knew that death was certain. There had been guys who wanted to kill me, but wanting to kill me and taking action to make it a reality were two different things.

These death squads were no joke. They were highly active on this compound. Within 30 days we had seen 29 people get stabbed. Nearly every day, someone was getting carried out on a stretcher with more holes in them than when the day had started. If something didn't change, I would be the next guy on that stretcher.

Chapter 20

CONFRONTING A KILLER

Before I even opened my eyes, I began praying. I knew that today was going to require a lot of character traits that, in and of myself, I did not possess. The day before, I decided to give the entire situation to God. I knew that any decision involving me attempting to get my enemy before he got me would end in nothing but disaster. I was so close to having the opportunity to go home that I knew this was, in part, an attempt by the devil to prevent me from hitting the streets.

After my session of prayer, I got out of bed and did what I had to do in order to get ready for work. I walked to the factory and entered the building before the majority of the men had arrived. As I walked to the rear of the factory, I could see that someone was in my department, but I couldn't see who was there until I rounded the corner. Upon turning the bend I saw that Anthony was there—he was the only one there.

Tony was 6 feet 4 inches tall and weighed 275 pounds. I stand 5 feet 11 inches, and, at the time, I only weighed 155 pounds. He towered over me, and ordinarily, that wouldn't be an issue, but Anthony was mad.

I walked up to him. He was vibrating with rage. Every part of him was shaking with hate for me. Slowly I approached him and said, "Anthony, I know about the hit, and I have known since yesterday. Don't worry, I'm not going to rat you out. I'm not going to say anything to anybody, but I want you to know something. I have never done anything to jeopardize your job here. Matter of fact, the only reason that you are still working here is because I told Dee (our supervisor) that I would help train you. I want you to think about what will actually happen when the hit goes through. First, it won't give you the job security you need since you will continue to break needles and tear fabric unless you learn how to operate the machine. Secondly, if you think Dee won't find out what happened to me, you are sorely mistaken. Both you and I know that someone will eventually talk. I'm not going to beg you to take the hit off; I just want you to see me for who I really am. I have always been here to help you, and in spite of this, I always will be. If you need anything, feel free to ask. I would be more than willing to help you out."

And with that, I turned and walked away. I went to my machine and started the day as though it was like any other. The day was uneventful and so were the 13 days that followed it. The hit never came. I watched for it, but nothing happened. My prayers for safety continued and no hit squad came calling. When at work, I continued doing my job as though nothing had ever happened. I treated Anthony as though the situation between he and I had never been a life and death situation. The attitude within the department leveled out and life went on as it had for months. Then one day, something that I could have never foreseen came at me like a charging rhino.

Every day, we had a 15 minute break between the two four-hour sessions that we worked. The event happened during the morning break. Now, what you need to know is that during our breaks, I usually broke out my Bible in order to get in some extra reading. I wasn't supposed to have it in there, but I knew that my supervisor didn't mind.

I had my face in my Bible when Anthony pulled up a chair next to me. I closed my Bible and gave him a look of concern. Anthony had tears just rolling down his face. As he sat down, he put his face in his hands and just sobbed. Everyone around us watched but made an effort to appear as if they weren't. I put my hand on his shoulder and asked him if he was okay. He continued to sob, and after about 30 seconds, he composed himself and looked up with tear-filled eyes. He said, "I am so sorry, Greg. I just want to say I'm sorry."

I told him that his apology was accepted. He looked up from his hands again and said, "After that morning, told the guys that I was canceling the hit and they turned against me. I had been their friend for over ten years, but in one second they turned on me. They haven't spoken to me since then except to make comments about me. I had done a lot for those guys, but it was like none of that mattered."

Then, Anthony pulled something from his pocket that surprised me as few things have. It was a small Gideon's New Testament. He explained to me, "Over the last several months, I have been reading this." He then began quoting Scripture as though he was reading it word for word, but he wasn't reading from it. As he quoted the texts I marveled. Anthony had been memorizing the Bible on his own, knowing that it would not be considered "acceptable" by many of those that he associated with.

I was SHOCKED! I have been surprised before, but nothing had ever floored me as this had. Every stereotype that I had placed upon Anthony was crushed in one swift movement. Never again would I look at anyone or how God works through them the same again.

As Anthony quoted portions of Psalms and Proverbs, he told me what it meant to him. I saw in him the beauty of how the Holy Spirit works. God had been working on him as He had been working on me. The surrounding circumstances may have been different, but the results were the same. Was he perfect? No, but neither is anyone else. God is working with an imperfect canvas. The paint He uses may be flawless, but the canvas (us) that He is applying it to has some "rough spots." Anthony putting a hit out on me was the result of one of those "rough spots," but as he sat next to me, I saw someone whom God was drawing into a relationship with Himself.

The opportunity was not lost on me. I saw what God had brought us together for. I looked at Anthony and told him that he was welcome to join our weekly Bible study and worship hour. I knew what this would require of him. He would have to disavow his current religion and formally sign up for our Bible study group. To do so would essentially be the same as putting a hit out on himself. I told him that God was drawing him into a deeper knowledge of Himself and that He was clearly working within this situation. Anthony saw the wisdom in what I was saying but didn't say whether he was going to change his religious preference with the chaplain's office.

A week later, as I began organizing the chairs for the Bible study, I saw Anthony walking toward the programs building with Bible in hand. I immediately thanked God for His magnificent work in both of our lives. I had seen the power of God in my life, but to see it manifested in such a way in somebody else's was amazing. That evening, we studied the Bible and worshipped God together. Had you told me four weeks earlier what would be happening that night, I would have smiled and thought that you were either a little crazy or sampling someone else's medication. But there we were, praising God, and studying His Word together.

That evening, my heart was filled with joy, filled with the Holy Spirit, and filled with questions about how I could serve God in the future. If working for God meant that my life would be in jeopardy or even lost, if it meant that someone like Anthony would come to a saving relationship with Jesus Christ, then I was ready to walk that road. I had seen others express their faith in Christ before, but never had I seen someone risk their life to learn more about God. That was a life lesson well learned. Even now, it brings tears to my eyes. If only those who claim to be Christians could exercise such faith, the Spirit of God would be manifested as it was in the days of Pentecost.

I don't know where Anthony is at in his walk with God today, but what I do know is where he was at in his walk back then. Weeks after this incident, I saw the parole board and learned my fate. The parole board member showed no emotion as she read off the crimes that I had been convicted of. Once finished with that lengthy list, she then read off the report that had been compiled by the MDOC in regards to my time in prison. Unbeknownst to me, my unit officers and supervisors had all written positive reports concerning my conduct throughout the seven years, and those reports helped the board member make her decision.

As the interview continued, she asked me what my plans were, and since I had no idea what God was going to do, I simply told her that I had employment lined up and that entailed me working with James at the restaurant that I had managed before. I told her about Brenda and I planning on marrying and that my intention was to successfully complete parole and become a productive member of society.

She took a few minutes to look over all of the factors, and then she said, "I have decided to grant you your parole. The other two board members will have to sign off, but if they do, you will be home in February."

I was elated, as was my mother. She and several other members of my family had driven down in order to attend the meeting. My mother had been there through it all. She had been there through my years of rebellion and addiction, and she had been there through my incarceration as an active supporter. Whenever I needed a book to further my education, she would do what she could to make sure that I got it, and during those moments of exhaustion, she was there to encourage.

On February 8, 2012, I was released from G. Robert Cotton Correctional Facility, and my family was there to meet me as I walked out the door. So much had changed in my life. I had walked into prison alone and walked out surrounded by those that I had victimized. The relationships that I had destroyed, God had restored. The magnitude of the situation was not lost on me. I couldn't help but get choked up as I walked out of the prison. I knew that I would never walk back into the prison in the same capacity that I had entered it before.

Chapter 21

WITH GOD

hree days after I was released, Brenda and I were married in the courtroom of one of the judges who had once called me a "menace to society." We had weighed the idea of having a big wedding, but in the end we decided that simplicity was best. We didn't want to start our life together burdened by a bunch of debt. Our wedding only cost ten dollars, and the Justice of the Peace who officiated it had an excellent sense of humor and performed a beautiful ceremony. We left the courtroom and went to a restaurant across the street to eat a dinner with our parents and some of our loved ones.

Things were not easy to adjust to. I found myself extremely uncomfortable in crowds, and no matter where we sat down, I noticed that I always sat with my back up against the wall. I wasn't comfortable unless I could see my surroundings. I just couldn't seem to shake what I had been through. Three full days passed before I was able to fall asleep in my new surroundings. I had been sleeping in a battle zone for seven years, and now, trying to sleep in a quiet and peaceful environment was unnatural. On the fourth night, I finally collapsed in exhaustion.

Once I was settled, I went and spoke with James about the job offer, and it was then that he told me that due to the economy, there was no position open. It wasn't that he had to downsize; people just weren't taking their employment so casually anymore. He had been given no reason to let anyone go so until that occurred, there wouldn't be a spot for me.

At first, I was disappointed, but I remembered that God was always at work in the lives of those who were living for Him. I knew that He had something different in store if He hadn't preserved the job that I had lined up. Over the next couple of weeks, I discussed my lack of employment with several friends from church. In private conversations, every one of them, in spite of not having spoken with one another, said the same thing: "You should become a literature evangelist."

Up until this time, I had never heard of a literature evangelist. I began asking some of the leadership in our church what that position entailed, and they told me that a literature evangelist was someone who shared the gospel with strangers by utilizing Christian literature. This type of evangelist would go to the homes of individuals in the community, share their personal testimony of how these books have affected their lives, and then show them how they could experience similar results by applying the principles expressed in the literature. The books that they supplied were all designed to lead somebody to the Bible. In and of themselves, the books were powerless. Each book was specifically designed to encourage someone to pick up a Bible and begin studying the Word of God for themselves.

I was curious, so one afternoon I purchased some of the literature and began going from home to home. Before stepping foot toward any home, I would ask God to guide me and to give me the words to speak. I knew that this type of work was wholly dependent upon my relationship with God. Without that relationship, this job would be unsuccessful both monetarily and spiritually. Over the next few months, my work grew and grew.

Each day, I would come home with stories about how God had worked a miracle that day. It was amazing to see how God was working in the lives of the people that I encountered. There were days where I would give away a lot of literature and not make any money, but I knew that it was never about the money. The next day, God would reward. Somebody would feel inspired to donate extra funds to cover for someone who couldn't afford the books. In the end, it all worked out. My bills were paid, and my business continued to grow. Even today, nearly two years later, I am still receiving phone calls from people who are interested in more Christian literature, and these are people that I only had one brief encounter with.

As the months went by, I felt God calling me to alter how I shared what He had done in my life. I felt like it was time for me to begin working directly in the community that I had once victimized. I prayed about it and discussed what I was experiencing with my wife. After considering the situation, I decided to approach a local church with a proposal.

The church invited me to present my proposal, and that evening I told them how I felt God calling me to give back to the community that I had taken so much from. Even though I had been gone for nearly eight years, I could still see the negative effects of the work I had done as a drug dealer. I told the congregation that I felt God calling me to go throughout the community and connect with those who were looking for something to fill that God shaped hole in their lives. I wanted to share the very thing that had had such a profound effect on my life, I wanted to share the love of Christ. I explained how I believed Christ's love manifested itself in many ways, in showing people the beauty of God's Word, by helping them get through the difficult times in life, and by lending a helping hand with the tasks that nobody else makes themselves available for. I wanted to be a missionary in the town that I lived in.

After much consideration, the church agreed to hire me to be the missionary that I knew God was calling me to be. As a representative of the church, I offered my time, energy, and strength to those who were in need.

Within weeks, I was experiencing significant results from my efforts. About 20 people had made a decision to draw closer to God through a deeper study and application of His Word. I loved my job! I got to do the very thing that I loved to do. I could meet complete strangers and talk about God and get paid for it!

How different my life was from what I thought it was going to be. I remember the days where I thought that the only option that I had left was to commit suicide—that my life wasn't worth anything. I had become a drug addict of the worst kind. I had robbed both of my parents and had stolen from those who trusted me in order to support a habit that had resulted from my own choices. I thought that I had destroyed any potential that I possessed—and I had. But what I soon discovered was that it wasn't about what I possessed, it was about what Jesus Christ possessed. Success in life didn't depend on what I had done or could do, it was about what I would allow God to do through me.

What I saw was that when I gave God control of my life, the future was full of possibilities. All of the impossibilities that life could throw my way became possible because "all the promises of God in Him [Christ] are Yes," (2 Corinthians 1:20). There was nothing that couldn't happen if it was found in God's will. My past had no bearing as to whether or not something *could* happen.

When I go to prisons, or schools, life-groups or churches to speak, I make it abundantly clear that **your past does not have to dictate your future**. Our futures are only limited by our willingness to submit to God. He has the power and ability to make anything a reality. If you are a child of God and your will is centered in God's will, you can do all things through Christ who strengthens you

(Philippians 4:13). It doesn't matter whether you were a prostitute addicted to crack, a junky addicted to heroin, or a husband addicted to anger or pornography. The answer to every issue in life is found in Christ, and even though we may face difficulties in our walk, we will make it through those trials with a sense of peace because we will know that we have the most powerful person in existence standing in our corner.

I still face challenges in life. I am not perfect by any means. I continue to grow in Christ, and when I find that I have fallen in one aspect of my walk, I look to the One who I know can lift me from the pit that I have dug for myself. Without fail, He comes to my rescue by giving me the strength to not only stand again, but the strength to remain standing.

Friend, I don't know where you are today. I don't know whether you are at home, in a prison cell, or on the street, but what I do know is that no matter where you are in life, you have a Friend who loves you, a Friend who understands not only where you have been, but where you can be. I found that same Friend when I was in the deepest, darkest area in my life. I saw no way out but death, and had God not stepped in, I would have died. I would have prevented myself from ever experiencing the happiness that God wanted me to have, from ever sharing that happiness with others who are living in the same desperation that I had found myself in.

Today, I invite you to evaluate your current situation. If you would like to experience happiness, contentment, and peace through all of life's storms, I challenge you to make the most important decision of your existence; I challenge you to give up everything that you have ever dreamed of, wished for, and depended upon; to trust in Someone who knows you better than you know yourself, Someone who loves you more than anyone could ever love you. Give up and give your heart to Christ, for He says:

> I know the thoughts that I have toward you…thoughts of peace and not of evil, to give you a future and a hope. Then you will call upon Me … and I will listen to you. And you will seek Me and find Me, when you search for Me with all of your heart. I will be found by you … and I will bring you back from your captivity. (Jeremiah 29:11–14)

FINAL NOTE FROM THE AUTHOR:

I would like to dedicate this book to the memory of my mother Sheryl and my step-father Norm, my father Don and step-mother Ginger all of whom stuck with me in spite of all of the dirt that I did.

Secondly, I would like to thank my wife Brenda, who not only remained faithful in trial and tribulation, but has always provided a steady stream of love and wisdom. A special thank you goes out to Kevin Barrett, Don Clay, Larry Cruttenden, and Rick Collier— leadership at Riverside Fellowship—for giving me the opportunity to give back to the community that I once victimized. And finally, to Chief Bukala and the officers/staff at the Lowell Police Department for allowing me —a six-time convicted felon and then parolee—the opportunity to show those in my community that with God, a person can change.

Where Darkness Reigned,
Light Overcame!

Now is the TIME to Know

The Bible is as relevant as ever to your life and family. Let us prove it! Our Bible Study Guides will help you understand the Bible better than you ever have before ...

Find the answers you need!

Send for the printed guides absolutely FREE!

✂ -

Bible Correspondence Course
P.O. Box 426
Coldwater, MI 49036

Name _____

Address _____

City _____

State _____ ZIP _____

Phone (____) _____ Email _____

Free offer available in North America and U.S. territories only.

RP1188